You Can Get There from Here

A Lillenas Drama Resource

You Can Get There from Here

Featuring
"Warmwater, Illinois: The Youth Edition"
and other plays for teens

by Lawrence G. Enscoe
and Andrea J. Enscoe

Lillenas Publishing Company
Kansas City, MO 64141

Dedicated . . .

To our families, who brought us up in the way of the Lord. We did not depart. Thank you.

And, to Paul Miller, for his vision, exuberance, and good taste.

Contents

Preface

When Paul Miller first approached us about writing a book for teenagers about teenagers, we sat down to our first brainstorming session filled with ideas for humorous and lighthearted sketches.

Then we began talking with youth pastors about the spiritual and emotional lives of their young people. We heard statistics about suicide, casual sexual activities, sexual diseases, drug addiction, and apathetic spiritual lives that would give you an anxiety attack. And these were kids in the church. We realized that the kinder, gentler approach might not be what was needed, but rather a tough, realistic evaluation of the facts of life in our times.

So what follows is a collection of 21 sketches that we hope are honest, sobering, funny, sad, and memorable. There are plays that are specifically for church groups, and some are designed for evangelism. Some are meant to have fun with a gentle message. Some carry the sharp edges of the real world. We haven't pulled any punches, but it was also important for us to present these issues without intending to shame or judge. We haven't always opted for the nice ending, either. We win souls with the truth, not with a fantasy of what we wish life were like.

Nobody said it was going to be easy for teenagers in the 1990s. I think we can all agree on that. There are a lot of pressures. Our society thrives on telling lies to get us to participate in things that aren't healthy for us spiritually, emotionally, and physically. And teenagers are particularly vulnerable. They often don't have the perspective, the life experience, or the emotional stability to make the most life-enhancing choices. Adults barely have that one down themselves.

What we need now more than ever is to tell the truth to our teenagers about what they're up against and who's on their side. Not denial, not "if I don't tell them, they'll never find out about it," not "Oh, they'll get through it, I did." As it's said elsewhere in this book, what these young people don't know most certainly *will* hurt them.

We simply wanted to tell the truth: That what you've done can be healed and transformed by the saving grace of Jesus Christ. We make choices that aren't always healthy, because we don't know any better, because we've been lied to, or because we're just broken people. But here's the good news: You are not condemned to struggle through life alone. With the strength, grace, and comfort of Jesus, you'll be sure to get there from here.

Please prayerfully consider using what this collection has to offer. We believe it's a big step toward making the outstretched arm of the church more relevant and compelling.

LAWRENCE AND ANDREA ENSCOE
February 1990

A NOTE ABOUT SLANG

Nothing in life changes faster than slang. Please feel free to substitute the slang used in these sketches with whatever is running around your neighborhood at the time of production. You should do the same with the celebrities mentioned by name. Please keep us current.

WARMWATER, ILLINOIS
The Youth Edition
A Soap Opera in 10 Sketches

Myrtle Fetschwanger, that living, breathing example of the stuffy church lady, says it best in the opening sketch. After commenting that a group of teens hanging around a mall on Saturday afternoon are "slackers and loiterers," she rattles off a litany of criticism about their emotional selves. "Immature," she shouts. "Confused! Frightened! Impressionable! Vulnerable!"

Well, these aren't criticisms at all. They are the simple truth. Later, when the teenagers retort with, "But we're just kids!" they are met with, "If you're going to be kids, try doing it a little more like adults!"

The fact is, teenagers are not adults—even though they are met with the same temptations, the same questions, and the same issues as their grown-up counterparts.

You're going to meet a brother and sister who finally learn how to treat each other well, a boyfriend and girlfriend struggling with sexual boundaries, a youth group "core" that always ends up doing all the work, a young man working out how to make his parents' faith his own, and a trio of teens who are fighting a tumbling sense of self-esteem.

The play, the third in the continuing soap opera of Warmwater, Ill., a town of lukewarm Christians who don't "walk their talk," takes a gentle jab at what it means to be a teenager in the church today. The sketches that follow are meant to confront and challenge, often using satire, but in a spirit that also understands that young people are precious, valuable members of the Christian church body.

In the end, we agree with Muffy Stewart's closing words in the final sketch: "Youth group," she says. "Ya gotta love 'em. Ya just gotta!"

Well, yes you do.

Warmwater, Illinois

The Youth Edition

Running Time

65 minutes

Set

"Warmwater, Illinois: The Youth Edition" can be played in two possible ways. One direction to go is to use the background flats and skyline indicated in the script. This will offer entrance and exits and offstage space. The other way the play can be performed is on an open playing area with costumes and prop tables visible, so all characters and set changes take place in full view of the audience.

The "Warmwater" set is designed to be as detailed or slight as the performance team wants to make it.

Cast

Warmwater, Illinois was created for an entire youth group to take on as a performance project. The opening sketch, "Welcome to Warmwater," requires a cast of at least 14. The entire play can be done with 14 actors. See each sketch for individual cast requirements.

The ANNOUNCER, who sets up and closes many sketches, can be either performed live or on an offstage mike or tape. Also, where indicated, YOUTH GROUP TEENS can either be performed onstage or on tape.

The entire play can be performed by junior-high- and high-school-age actors. Three characters can be played either by adults or teens in makeup and older costumes. These are MYRTLE FETSCHWANGER, MAYOR STOKER, and YOUTH PASTOR.

Production Notes

STRUCTURE: There are several ways "Warmwater" can be performed or utilized. First of all, the 10 sketches (11 with opening) can be done straight through in a full program of both serious and comic looks at being a Christian teenager. This format will make it difficult to have meaningful discussion and teaching after each segment.

The second option is to simply pull out the sketches you want to do. Each sketch—except the opening—was written to stand on its own to augment discussion in a youth group or youth and parents meeting.

OPENING
Welcome to Warmwater

"Warmwater" Young People (entire cast)
Myrtle Fetschwanger
Mayor Stoker
Youth Pastor
Announcer
Scene: the John Wyclif Memorial Mall and a youth pastor's office

(In the darkness, we hear some techno-pop music [no lyrics]. This goes on for a few moments, then the lights come up to reveal an old-fashioned lamppost, down left. The attached street sign reads "Complacent Corners." An upstage flat [or two separate flats] stretches across the playing area. There is an entrance in the middle of the flat. The skyline of a typical Midwestern town can be seen beyond the flat. An arched wooden sign across the top of the flat reads: "The Most Spiritual Little City in the World." The playing area has two benches, several potted plants, and a free-standing sign that reads: "John Wyclif Memorial Mall. Hours 10 A.M. to 9 P.M."

(After a moment, in come the Young People—the cast of the play. They are dressed to represent the wide range of American youthdom—jocks, nerds, dudes, long-hairs, etc. They carry shopping bags, Walkmans, backpacks, skateboards, etc. They swarm onstage: talking, laughing, walking in rhythm, high fives, hip handshakes, and waves. Their exuberance builds.

(Suddenly, Myrtle Fetschwanger strides in with Mayor Stoker in tow, wearing his trademark overcoat, ascot, and glasses.)

Myrtle: There they are!

(The mall soundtrack screeches to a halt. The Young People all turn to Myrtle in surprise, confusion, amusement, and attitude.)

Young People *(in greeting)*: Yo!

Myrtle: There they all are, Mayor Stoker!

Mayor: It's a whole gang of 'em!

Young People: Us?!

MYRTLE: Yes, yes! YOUNG PEOPLE! Look at them all. Loitering around the mall! Nothing to do! Wasting time! Growing up!

YOUNG PEOPLE: But it's summer!

MYRTLE: Look at their posture. The way they dress! The way they act!

MAYOR: The way they mangle English!

YOUNG PEOPLE: Like, totally!

MYRTLE: Forever saying, "yo" and "dude" and "full-on way radical!"

YOUNG PEOPLE: You forgot "Groovy!" "Cat's pajamas!" and "Bee's knees!"

MYRTLE: They're bein' smart, Mayor!

MAYOR: You were sassin' Myrtle Fetschwanger here!

YOUNG PEOPLE: Nuh-uh!

MYRTLE: Haul 'em in! Haul 'em in!

YOUNG PEOPLE: For what?!

MYRTLE: For . . . for . . . for—

MAYOR: For being too old to spank and too young to vote!

YOUNG PEOPLE: You mean, for being a teenager?

MAYOR/MYRTLE: That's right!

YOUNG PEOPLE: But it's not our fault!

MYRTLE: Slackers! Loiterers! Loud voices! Loud colors! Immature! Confused! Frightened! Impressionable! Vulnerable!

YOUNG PEOPLE: But we're just—

MAYOR: KIDS! We know, we know! Well, let me tell you something. If you're going to be kids, TRY DOING IT A LITTLE MORE LIKE ADULTS!

(The YOUNG PEOPLE *all turn to the audience with mouths open in amazement and confusion. All freeze.*)

ANNOUNCER (*offstage*): Ladies and gentlemen! . . . and young people. And now for another edifying episode with the folks at . . . (*a melodramatic glissando on the organ*) . . . Warmwater, Illinois!

(*The mall soundtrack takes over and the* YOUNG PEOPLE *start moving and talking as before.*)

MYRTLE: Stop that! Stop that . . . that . . . that NOISE!

(*The music stops. The* YOUNG PEOPLE *stop. A soundtrack of E. Power Biggs' [or someone's] favorite organ tunes begins. The* YOUNG PEOPLE *groan en masse and pop on Walkman headphones.* MAYOR STOKER *and* MYRTLE FETSCHWANGER *mix in with them, fixing posture, adjusting clothes, and pulling headphones out of ears.)*

ANNOUNCER: Ah, Warmwater! That happy, blessed town, where all people live in one accord. Yes, come to Warmwater, where almost everyone believes what you do . . . and where there hasn't been a major sin for over 30 years! Yes, folks, tune in and hear the mayor say:

MAYOR *(grabbing at headphones):* Take those off, you twerp! That had better be Bill Gaither in there! *(Notices the audience)* Ah . . . howdy, folks. Why, we'd just love for you to come to Warmwater. *(Looks away)* Go home and patch those britches, mister! *(To audience)* Ah, providin' you're a Christian, that is. *(Away at a girl carrying videotape boxes)* That better be *Bambi* and *Focus on the Family,* missy! *(To audience)* And if you're not a Christian . . . well, you had better JUST PASS RIGHT ON THROUGH! *(Everyone stops. Silence.* MAYOR *smiles and chuckles.)* Well, all right. Should you decide to stay here in Warmwater, yet, why you can just . . . act like you're a Christian! We don't want to make any waves. *(Winks)* You understand.

YOUNG PEOPLE: WORD!

(Blackout. The organ continues playing background music.)

ANNOUNCER: It's now September here in beautiful, blessed, benevolent Warmwater.

(Lights. A young man enters carrying a bucket with sponges, a box of buttermilk pancake mix, videos, books, tracts, calendars, handouts, a backpack, skis, and a paint can. This is YOUTH PASTOR. *He sits on a bench and begins sorting through and checking everything on a list. He's getting visibly more distraught.)*

ANNOUNCER: The long, humid summer is over here in God's favorite little burg. The days are getting shorter, the *TV Guide* has announced this year's newest round of ungodly programs, and heaven has already begun showing its rainbow of colors in the elms, the oaks, and Fanny Vandersma's hair.

YOUTH PASTOR: Where are the peewee golf announcements! THE PEEWEE GOLF ANNOUNCEMENTS!

ANNOUNCER: For the churches here in pre-Trib Warmwater, it is surely a joyous time of the year! Pastors are busy shoring up their fall sermon titles, church pews are beginning to fill up, the new Sunday School material has just arrived, and Mrs. Fingerworthy, the one and only pianist over at Pastor Dorcas's church, has just returned from an 11-week tour of The Old Country that she didn't bother telling the choir director she was going on.

VOICE *(offstage):* Let me at her! Let me at her!

YOUTH PASTOR *(looking off and calling):* Anybody seen the gorp and ski-trip lift

16

tickets? Ah! No! Where's the Russ Taff CDs! The Brown songbooks! My guitar! MY GUITAR!

ANNOUNCER: Yes, everyone is buzzing with excitement at what the Lord's going to do this year! Except for this man. You see, he's a special breed of servant here in Warmwater. He's what's known as a . . . youth pastor. And, for him, September means only one thing.

YOUTH PASTOR *(throwing up some handouts in panic)*: YOOUUNG PEEEOOOPLE!

(Blackout. The organ music continues.)

ANNOUNCER: Yes, well, it's Wednesday night here in sweet, sacred, eternally secure Warmwater. And we all know what that means. Yes, indeed, it's mid-week church. Come on down to any church in Warmwater and you'll find teenagers—lots of teenagers—attending youth groups all across town. *(The organ music stops. We hear the sounds of voices building.)* Why, look, we're in luck. Tonight is the kickoff program for the school year. Let's just take a peek and see what Warmwater's loving, spiritual, and tenderhearted youth are up to now.

SKETCH 1

Tongues

DUDE 1
DUDE 2
DUDE 3   all junior-high- and/or high-school-age
GIRL 1
GIRL 2
GIRL 3
GUITAR PLAYER (offstage or on tape)
SCENE: a youth group room

(Lights on three DUDES, sitting in chairs, holding Bibles and handouts. They're checking out the new youth group scene. Three GIRLS on the opposite side of the playing area are doing the same thing. At the moment, the GIRLS are frozen, heads bowed and in the dark.)

DUDE 1: Look at that zit on Kerry! It's massive. Gotta be as big as Kansas!

DUDE 2: Get a clue, dude. It's pizza sauce on her face, not an eruptoid.

DUDE 3: From the size of her I'd say she's been eatin' lots'a pizzas. All summer.

DUDE 1: Yo, just think how big she'd be if she'd actually got the pizza in her mouth.

(They laugh. One of them looks up.)

DUDE 2: Who me? Ah . . . sure, Pastor Dave. *(They all bow their heads.)* Lord, ah . . . just thank You for gettin' us all here safe. And . . . ah . . . thanks for You, and . . . help us to hear Your Word tonight. Help us to serve You better. Ah . . . in Your name we pray—

(Lights out on the DUDES and up on the GIRLS, who bring up their heads out of prayer.)

GIRL: Amen.

GIRL 1: Hey, isn't that Jim Collins.

GIRL 2: Yeah, so what.

GIRL 3: I thought you were going out with him over the summer.

GIRL 2: The dude's a loser.

GIRL 1: Who is that bim he's with? Hey, that's Marion Schmidt!

GIRL 2: Yeah, big deal.

GIRL 3: You're way cuter, anyways. Massively. He's a geek.

GIRL 2: Yeah, and she's a toad.

GIRLS 1 & 3: Totally.

(Guitar begins playing a familiar chorus. The GIRLS look at their handouts.)

GIRLS *(singing)*: Have you seen Jesus, my Lord, He's here in plain view [or similar].

(Lights out on GIRLS and up on the DUDES, who are singing.)

DUDES: Take a look, open your eyes, He'll show it to you.

(The guitar stops. The DUDES look out.)

DUDE 2 *(pointing)*: Check it out. I don't believe it. Lawrence Simpson has a letter jacket on. From Calvin High, no less. No, over there. See 'im? Unbelievable.

DUDE 3: Get out. How'd that wimpazoid get a LETTER!

DUDE 1: No justice in high school. Simp the Wimp got a letter. It's over, dudes.

DUDE 2: Clue in, Holmes. The geek probably got it for outstanding service in the science club.

DUDE 1: Getting 10 straight A's on his biology tests.

DUDE 3: Or for best makeup in the school play.

DUDE 2: They hand those things out now to any dorknoid.

DUDES: No doubt. *(They look up, smile, and look enthusiastic.)*

DUDES: Give me a J! Give me an E! Give me an S! Give me a U! Give me an S! What's that spell?!

(Blackout on the DUDES. Lights up on the GIRLS.)

GIRLS: JESUS! JESUS! JEEESSSUUUSSS! *(They applaud.)*

GIRL 3: I can't believe it. *(Buries her face in friend's shoulder, groaning.)*

GIRLS 1 & 2: What?

GIRL 3: Carla Michaels. Over there! *(They look.)*

GIRL 1: Bad news.

GIRL 2: Looks like Jenny Craig flunked her big-time.

GIRL 3: She got gi-huge-ic. Least she could do is spare us all and stop dressing like a size 3. That is scary.

GIRL 2: Her mom should take her out and buy her a new wardrobe.

GIRL 1: Yeah. All black sweats. *(They laugh.)*

GIRL 3: Look, Mark Vanderhoff is still dating her! Isn't he varsity quarterback this year. I wonder what she's doing to keep a bohunk like that.

GIRL 2: Who knows. All I can say is that relationship is on a major skid if I ever saw one.

GIRL 1: And she told me she was going to try out for cheerleader this year.

GIRL 3: Fat chance. *(They laugh. GIRLS 1 and 3 do a high five. They stop.)*

GIRL 3: Ah, sure, Pastor Dave. Chapter what? *(Motions for GIRL 1's Bible. She opens and reads.)* "Consider what a great forest is set on fire by a small spark. The tongue also is a fire, a world of evil among the parts of the body."

(Blackout on the GIRLS. Lights up on the DUDES.)

DUDE 3 *(reading):* "With the tongue we praise our Lord and Father, and with it we curse men, who have been made in God's likeness. Out of the same mouth come praise and cursing. My brothers, this should not be." *(Closes the Bible. He looks up, and his eyes get big.)* Dudes, do you see what I see just walkin' in?

DUDE 2: She has gotta be new. What a babe. I don't see her with anyone, do you?

DUDE 1: She's walking this way. *(To* DUDE 3*)* I think she's lookin' at you, dude. Say somethin', say somethin'!

DUDE 3 *(cocky)*: Babe, you could sit over here next to me. *(He watches her pass.)* Can you believe that?

DUDE 2: The freeze out. She didn't even look at you. What a major bim!

DUDE 1: Aw, maybe she's just shy. She's new.

DUDE 3: Are you kiddin'? That's an Icee on two legs if I ever saw one.

DUDE 2: Major stuck-up. Blow her off. You wouldn't get nowhere with her anyway.

DUDE 3: I wouldn't even try.

DUDE 1: Yeah, she can just sit all by herself with an attitude like that!

(An offering plate passes down the line. They all drop change into it. The last DUDE *hands it off into blackout. Lights on the* GIRLS, *the first taking the plate and passing it down, dropping in change like the others.)*

GIRL 2: Right on cue. Look at that, Pastor Dave asks a question about the Bible and Ralph Bozer's got his hand up. He thinks he's the major brain of the universe.

GIRL 1: Give 'im a break. He's gotta be smart with a honker like his. What else has he got goin' for 'im?

GIRL 3 *(almost loud enough to be heard)*: Honk . . . honk!

GIRL 1: Can you imagine trying to kiss him?

GIRLS 2 & 3: Ewwww!

GIRL 3: Check it out, you'd have to have your pilot's license to get around his nose!

GIRL 2: Gaggers!

GIRL 1: Yeah, he'd sure better thank God that He gave him brains.

(The lights suddenly come up on both sides of the stage.)

GIRL 3: Come on. Closing song.

DUDE 3: Gotta stand, dudes.

(All stand. They hold out their song sheets to sing. The guitar starts playing, off. Suddenly, both sides see each other. They stare for a minute, offer a weak smile, and quickly look away.)

GIRLS/DUDES: LOOK AT THEM! THEY'RE STARING AT US! (*Both sides steal a quick glance at each other and turn away.*) THEY'RE TALKING ABOUT US! NO DOUBT! HOW RUDE!

(*Each one turns away, talking to the audience.*)

GIRL 1: I'll bet they can see this massive zit on my face from here.

DUDE 1: They're talkin' about my nose again. I can feel it.

GIRL 2: They can see those doughnuts on me. I just know they're calling me "thunder thighs" right now.

DUDE 2: They're laughin' at me. I know it. This stupid haircut. My mom, I could kill 'er.

GIRL 3: They're wonderin' why I never get a date. They prob'ly think I'm way desperate. That I'll do whatever it takes. I wouldn't!

DUDE 3: They prob'ly thought I was lookin' at 'em. Like I was interested or somethin'. They think I'm some kind'a dork. I'm such a jerk.

(*The guitar stops. Silence.*)

GIRLS/DUDES: WHY DO THEY HAVE TO NOTICE ME? WHY DO THEY HAVE TO TALK ABOUT ME? DON'T THEY KNOW HOW I FEEL?

(*Blackout. The organ begins playing soft background music.*)

ANNOUNCER: Youth group. That strange and wonderful collection of near-perfect teenagers who always have great self-esteem, always know the right thing to do, and always put Jesus first in their lives. Just like their parents. What a special place. Right now, we're going to take a peek at some more of Warmwater's exceptional young people. Meet Rich, Rand, and Ashleigh, who are just out for the typical, wholesome American meal. Except, funny thing, one of them . . . just isn't hungry.

(*In the darkness we hear restaurant noises—people laughing, talking, silverware and glasses tinkling, faint music.*)

SKETCH 2
Off the Menu

RICH
RAND   all high-school-age
ASHLEIGH
WAITRESS
SCENE: a coffee shop

(ASHLEIGH, RAND, *and* RICH *are sitting around a coffee shop table. They're laughing.*)

RAND: No way. Get out, Rich. I'm not letting you have one, get it, not one of my french fries. You always embarrass me when you stick 'em up your nose and play Count Snotula.

RICH: One time! One time! Ashleigh, tell 'im. One time I did the Snotula gig, and now I can never get a fry out've the guy.

ASHLEIGH: I'm out. I'm outta this. You two can stick food in your ears if you want, just leave me out of it. That is exactly why I ordered a cheese sandwich. You can't do anything gross with a cheese sandwich. (RAND *and* RICH *look at each other and laugh.*)

RAND: Oh no? One time Rich—

ASHLEIGH: Shut up, Rand! I don't even want to hear about it!

RICH: Check it out. You're gonna get a pickle spear, right? With your sandwich. (RAND *breaks out laughing.*)

ASHLEIGH: I'm afraid to say yes.

RAND: One time Rich here rolled up the pickle spear and stuck it in his mouth. When the waitress came up—this way, squirrelly waitress—Rich opens his mouth to say something, and this pickle flops out. Like it was his tongue or something. It hits the table, right? The waitress sees it and loses it. She dumps it right there. Rich is holdin' the pickle spear and screamin', "Get a doctor! Get a doctor!"

RICH: My best work. My best!

ASHLEIGH: Remind me never to invite you two over for dinner.

RICH: Aw, we're housebroken.

(*The* WAITRESS *comes up carrying two plates and shake glasses.*)

WAITRESS: OK, the cheese sandwich—?

ASHLEIGH: Here.

WAITRESS: And french dip and fries.

RAND: Yeah. (WAITRESS *sets the plates down.* RICH *looks at* ASHLEIGH'*s plate.*)

ASHLEIGH: Do not touch my pickle. (RICH *holds his hands up innocently.*)

WAITRESS: That it?

RAND: Think so.

WAITRESS: What about you, Rich? You don't want anything? *(Small pause)*

RICH *(flips open his menu):* I don't think so right now. I'll keep looking, though. (*The* WAITRESS *smiles and goes out.*) I'm not very hungry yet, I guess.

ASHLEIGH: You must come here a lot.

RICH: Sometimes. Why?

ASHLEIGH: 'Cuz she knew your name. I don't see a name tag on you anywhere.

RICH: Who? Oh, the waitress? She goes to school with us.

ASHLEIGH: I've never seen her.

RAND: Ditto.

ASHLEIGH: Rand would'a already asked her out if she did.

RAND: No doubt.

RICH *(suddenly irritated):* She's in my algebra class, OK? Mrs. Culbertson. 2:10. Room 245. You want a signed affadavit?

ASHLEIGH *(surprised):* No. Sheesh!

RICH *(after a moment, he reaches for* RAND'*s fries):* Mind if I—? (RAND *holds up his fork to protect them.*) Fine. (RICH *pouts.* ASHLEIGH *rolls her eyes and hands him a couple of fries. He wolfs them, then looks at his watch.*) So. You two be heading off to youth group at seven, huh?

ASHLEIGH: Yeah.

RAND: Just like every Wednesday.

ASHLEIGH: You think you might want to come with us this time?

RICH *(laughs):* What, are you kidding?

RAND: Just like every Wednesday.

RICH: Aren't you cute. *(Looks off)* Isn't that Ferret-Face Ferguson over there? What's he doin' out of his chem lab? (*The other two look off.* RICH *whips a couple of fries off* RAND'*s plate.*) Ya never learn, doof.

RAND: I hate it when you pull that! Why don't you just order something for yourself?

RICH: I told you. I'm not hungry. I only want a taste, OK? I'm sorry, Wally. Yer not gonna fink to Dad, are ya? (RAND *is ticked big-time.*) OK, I'm sorry. Rand? Rand, c'mon. I won't do it again, all right? C'mon. Kiss me and make up, OK? (*Makes kissey*) Rand. Don't be a geek. (*Small pause. Another tactic.*) Hey, remember Mrs. Hayfever in third grade Sunday School?

ASHLEIGH (*tension laughter*): Mrs. Hayfever?

RAND: Hayfley. Her name was Mrs. Hayfley.

RICH: Every time she turned around we use'ta turn all the people upside down on her flannel board. You know those, like, cartoon Bible people on those flannel boards?

RAND (*to* ASHLEIGH): Here we go again. (*To* RICH) Yeah, I remember.

RICH: Somebody'd ask Hayfever some stupid question like: "Why'd the Israelites build a golden cow and not a golden Chihuahua?" or something big-time dumb, and while she looked it up in that huge children's Bible, we'd all—

RAND: —*you'd* all.

RICH: OK, I'd switch all the figures around. Turn all the sheep and goats and stuff upside down. Make the disciples do the rumba. Make a sheep bite Moses on his rear. Hang Zacchaeus from his feet out of the sycamore tree.

ASHLEIGH (*laughing*): That's terrible! Why'd you—?

RICH: For fun! We were bored.

RAND: You were bored.

RICH: All right, Mr. Sweet-and-Innocent, I was bored. Anyway, she'd get back to her lecture, and she's all . . . (*trembly, nasally voice*) "And then Jesus looked up in the tree and said—ZACCHAEUS! What happened to Zacchaeus?!" (*Sings*) "Zacchaeus, you come down, for I'm going to your house today!"

ASHLEIGH: That poor lady. She still goes to our church? Does she even talk to you guys?

RAND: She died a couple've years ago.

RICH: Man, kill the laugh track, why don'cha, Rand. Look, I'm not going to tell any more stories if Mr. Chuckles over here isn't going to join in.

RAND: I'm tired'a the stories, OK, Rich. Every time I see you now all you do is tell church stories and make fun've everything.

RICH: Can I help it if I've got a good eye for comedy? I see the humor in things. Maybe I'll be the next Jay Leno.

RAND: I'm glad you think my church and what I believe in is such a crack-up.

RICH: What *you* believe in? Suddenly I'm an atheist or something because I tell a couple'a jokes!

ASHLEIGH: Come on, you guys—

RAND: I didn't say that, Rich. It's just . . . Well, I don't know what you think about church. You're so hacked off at the whole place all you can do is make jokes. I feel like, it's either show up or shut up.

ASHLEIGH *(laughing)*: That's just Rand's bizarre way of inviting you to youth group.

RICH: Whoa. Let me find my car keys. I can't wait.

ASHLEIGH: I, for one, think youth group is great. We just went through this series on forgiveness that totally blew me out—

RICH: Really? Well, to an ex-stoner I guess that's pretty cataclysmic stuff, huh? When you finally get to the "Tell Me Something I Don't Know" series, then you can buzz my beeper. Until then, I'll keep my distance, thank you.

RAND: Lighten up, dork.

RICH: Look, my parents have got my Sundays, OK? Sewn up. Locked down. Sunday mornings, Sunday nights, I move with the flock. I couldn't stay home from church if my brains were leaking outta my eyes. Wednesday nights they can just . . .

WAITRESS *(entering with a coffeepot)*: Everyone OK over here?

RICH *(under his breath)*: Depends on who you ask, doesn't it?

WAITRESS: What's that?

ASHLEIGH: We're fine.

WAITRESS: Good enough. Rich, you made up your mind on anything?

RICH: Nothing right now.

WAITRESS: Good enough. *(She goes out.)*

ASHLEIGH: So where does your mom think you're going every Wednesday night?

RAND: To youth group.

RICH: That's right. And that's just where she better think I'm going, got it!

ASHLEIGH: Where do you go for three hours?

RAND: He sits right here. Every Wednesday night. He's so ticked at his parents he'll do anything to spite 'em. Sittin' here all by himself, suckin' up Diet Cokes.

RICH: That's my business. Just forget I said anything about it.

25

ASHLEIGH: It's weird. I couldn't get my parents to come to church if my life depended on it. They wouldn't even come to my baptism. Yours want you to go.

RICH: Order me to go.

ASHLEIGH: Why don't you just tell 'em how you feel?

RICH: My parents? What, and die? I can see it! *(Headline)* "Young Man Beaten to Death with King James Bible, Red-Letter Edition." *(Pause. He takes a breath.)* Look, church doesn't mean anything to me, OK? It's all what they want me to believe! It's like when I was six years old and we'd go into a restaurant and they'd tell me what I could have. *(Mother's voice)* "Oh, look here, Ritchie, a hot dog and fries! That's what you want, isn't it? Ah, Miss, Little Ritchie here'll have the hot dog and fries."

RAND: Come on, Rich. We're not talking about food here. We're talking about what you believe. Jesus and a hot dog are not the same thing—

RICH *(ignoring him)*: Hey, you gonna eat the rest'a that cheese sandwich, Ashleigh?

RAND: Rich? Rich? Captain Kirk to Rich? Listen to me this once, will you? Don't blow off God just because your parents believe—

RICH *(to ASHLEIGH)*: If you're just going to leave it, I'll—

RAND *(grabs ASHLEIGH's plate)*: That's it! Dude, that's your gig, isn't it? You're always lookin' on other people's plates to see what they got. You'll even take a taste, right? But you refuse to order anything for yourself.

RICH *(imitating RAND)*: A cheese sandwich and Jesus are not the same thing, Rand. (RAND *stares at him for a moment, then shakes his head. He sets the plate down.)*

RAND: Time to look at a menu, Rich. *(He stands.)* We're late. *(Grabs the check)* Let's jam, Ashleigh. *(He goes out.)*

ASHLEIGH: He's worried about you, that's all. He's your friend, Rich. You sure you won't come with, huh? (RICH *says nothing.)* Maybe next week. See ya. *(She goes out.)*

RICH *(calling after them)*: If you see my parents, you better zip it, Rand. *(He sits, staring ahead. He looks over at ASHLEIGH's plate. He pulls it over to him and picks up the sandwich, then sets it back down. Shoves the plate away. He opens the menu, looks at it a minute, then closes it. The WAITRESS comes up.)*

WAITRESS: Your friends leave?

RICH: Yeah. They went to church.

WAITRESS: Oh, that's nice. Wish I could go to church. Seems I always get stuck working on Wednesday nights and Sunday mornings. (*Pause. She points at the dishes.*) You want me to clear all that stuff away?

RICH: Sure. It's not mine.

WAITRESS: OK. (*She picks up the plates.* RICH *is looking off, distracted.*) You decided on anything?

RICH (*coming back*): What?

WAITRESS: Do you want something for yourself?

(*Pause.*)

RICH (*sighs*): I sure do.

(*The lights fade to:*)

(*Blackout.*)

ANNOUNCER: We shall return to lovely, lively, legalistic Warmwater in just a moment. But, first, a word from our sponsor.

SKETCH 3

School Witnessing Survival Kit: A Commercial

PITCHMAN (can be doubled by ANNOUNCER)
STUDIOUS GIRL
MR. BANZAI
HUNK   all junior-high- and/or high-school-age
MISSIONETTE
JUSTA GUY
THUMPER
SCENE: a school campus

(*The lights find a* STUDIOUS GIRL *sitting on a bench. She is reading an open book on her lap and has several others stacked next to her.*)

PITCHMAN (*off*): Ladies and gentlemen, does your witnessing have that . . . Carl Lewis flair to it?

(*Suddenly, we hear "BANZAIII" yelled and then someone blasts by* STUDIOUS GIRL, *dropping something in her lap and dashing off. She picks up the object—it's a tract. She looks at it, looks right and left, and finally straight up to heaven, wide-eyed. She freezes. We hear a loud piano tremolo. The* PITCHMAN *bounds in, dressed like a tacky, outrageous, used-car salesman. He sets a table down next to him covered with items.*)

PITCHMAN: Or maybe your evangelism style is a little like this?

(HUNK *walks in, carrying his books.* MISSIONETTE, *wearing a pith helmet, backpack, and jungle boots, follows behind.*)

HUNK: Look, I really don't know about this.

MISSIONETTE: No, no, it'd be great! See, we could go out to church and then do something afterward. Or to ice cream and then youth group. Or to pizza and a Bible study.

HUNK: I'm just not sure I—

MISSIONETTE: It'd be incredible! Check it out. You could go out with me, and you could get saved. What more could you ask for?

HUNK: Well . . . I like the getting saved part. It's going out with you I'm not crazy about. *(They freeze.)*

PITCHMAN: Ouch! Now that has gotta hurt. (JUSTA GUY *walks in and sits down, opening his lunch.* THUMPER *sits next to him and does the same.*) Or, maybe you're just tired of all these subtle routines and you want something with a little more punch. (THUMPER *opens his jean jacket, pulls out a Bible the size of Kansas, and baps* JUSTA GUY *over the head.* JUSTA GUY *goes cross-eyed and crashes to the floor, bologna sandwich in hand.*) Wow. Brutal. Nobody said sharing the Good News wasn't going to hurt a little, hmmmm? Oh, I know it's hard to tell that old gospel story without looking like a geek. I mean, how do you break the ice? How do you know what to say? Or, worst of all, how can you talk about Jesus and still maintain that massive-rad-dude-of-the-known-universe image? I know. I've worked hard to come up with my own tres natural, inoffensive style! And now you can, too, with Nerdman's "School Witnessing Survival Kit!" *(Laughs)* Oh, yes! With Nerdman's you'll never have to go it alone and say something dorky like: "Jesus knows what you're going through," "Say, Eunice, if you died tonight . . . ," and the ever popular, "Yo . . . Jesus, you. Word." *(He takes items off the table.)* Let's just take a peekaboo at what you get inside. First there's the ultra-hip "Look Out World, I'm a Christian" jean jacket and matching backpack and "Time for Jesus" wristwatch. There's also some special accessories to this basic ensemble—like this football helmet with the words "Jesus Heals" printed right in front. Ha! Those are the last words that wimpy quarterback'll see before the lights go out. *(Laughs)* How much would you really expect to pay for all this? But wait! There's more! If you order today, we'll send you this combination tract holder and portable CD player! It comes complete with alphabetized tracts on every subject, including "How to Share Jesus with the Wrestling Coach Who Breaks Clipboards over His Face" and "The Bible, Acne, and You." Think I'm done? You're way out of it! If you order today, you'll also get this outrageous two-way Walkman. Incredible! You can listen to Motley Crue and Guns n' Roses on the inside, while the outside is blaring Josh McDowell to the entire cafeteria! But don't touch that phone! We'll also send you this combination organizer binder and pop-up "Last Judgment" scene! Complete with wailing sinners and places to put yearbook photos of your pagan friends! We'll also put inside this free booklet, "101 Places for Unstoppable Witnessing." In it you'll discover incredible locations where you can find a captive audience—like during SAT exams, and in the bathroom stalls before finals! Now, how much would you expect to pay for all this? $100? $200? Fifty cents? But wait. If you order within the next 10 minutes, you'll also get a copy of the "Way Living Bible, Dude"—a contemporary transliteral approximation of the New Testament especially for teens! Here's John 1:1. "Like way back. Totally in the beginning and stuff there was the, Yo, Word. And Yo, the Word was hanging with God, and the, like, Yo, Word was God. Totally." Well, now you've got the complete package. How much can you get all this for? How about the outrageously low price of $39.99 with a letter from your parents saying you smashed all your cassettes except the Amy Grant tapes they bought you for Christmas. You can order by phone today. Just have Mom and Dad's credit card number ready. Remember, these items are not available in any store. Only through this amazing TV offer! The address is: Spewed Associations! Fourteen Forty-two Complacent Corners! Warmwater, Illinois! Six-Oh, Six-Oh Nine! Once again, that address is:

STUDIOUS GIRL/MR. BANZAI/HUNK/MISSIONETTE/JUSTA GUY/THUMPER: SPEWED ASSOCIATIONS! FOURTEEN FORTY-TWO COMPLACENT CORNERS! WARMWATER, ILLINOIS! SIX-OH, SIX-OH, NINE!!!

PITCHMAN: Yo, thanks.

ALL: NO DOUBT!

(Blackout.)

ANNOUNCER: Well, the school year is just speeding past here in Warmwater. Homecoming Sunday, peewee golfing, Splash Mountain, Skate-O-Rama, and 15 pancake breakfasts. All have come and gone. And now, it's almost Christmas, and the town is filling up with homesick college students returning to waiting, teary-eyed families. Let's check in with Zanny—who's about to get one "Ho, Ho, Ho!" of a Christmas present from her big brother.

SKETCH 4

The Brother from Another Planet

ZAN: a junior-high- or young high-school-age girl
BEN: a high-school- or college-age guy
SCENE: a family dining room

(Morning. A kitchen table and four chairs. ZAN comes in wearing a bathrobe and slippers, hair wild, and she's very groggy. She carries a box of cereal, milk, a bowl and spoon, and a handful of Equal packages. She sits, pours the cereal and milk, and begins to add in more Equal than any human should consume. She eats for a moment, reading the cereal box. She smiles suddenly and sticks her hand in the box, digging around for whatever schlocky prize awaits inside. She sees the audience. She smiles wanly and pulls her hand out, wiping it on her robe. She leans forward.)

ZAN *(conspiratorially)*: There's somethin' strange going on around here. Full-on bizarreness. *(She goes back to eating her cereal, hiding her face as she reads the cereal box. After a moment.)* I mean, what would you do if your brother came home from college and all'a sudden, he's the big brother you always wanted?

(She looks off, quickly. Someone's coming. She whips back to eating and reading the cereal box. Small pause. BEN comes in wearing 501s, a pullover, and Reeboks. He carries a bowl, a spoon, a glass, and a copy of the New York Times.*)*

BEN: Hey, Zanny. How'd you sleep? *(ZAN chokes on her cereal. She looks up at BEN, wide-eyed in disbelief.)*

ZAN: Uh . . . fine. Yeah . . . OK.

BEN: Great. *(ZAN asides an aghast look at the audience. BEN sits, opens the paper.)*

ZAN: Uh . . . you sleep OK?

BEN: Well, it's hard to get used to down mattresses and clean sheets when you've been sleeping on dorm pallets and you never do the laundry.

(ZAN laughs a short, very fake guffaw. BEN smiles and goes back to the paper. ZAN watches him for a minute, then waves a hand in front of him as if he might be hypnotized. BEN looks up from his paper.)

BEN: What are you doing?

ZAN *(twisting her hand in the air)*: Wrist exercises. I'm thinkin' about trying out for drum major.

BEN: Incredible, Zan. That's wild. Let me know if I can help you. I think I re-member some of the old routines from when I was in band. *(He goes back to reading. ZAN grabs her chest and falls back in her chair. She stares at him. Then at the audience. She shakes her head.)*

ZAN *(exaggerated mouthing):* It's not him . . . It's not—

BEN: You OK, Sis?

ZAN *(spinning around):* Yeah! Uh. When you start reading the paper? You only used t'read "Spiderman" at breakfast.

BEN: You pick up a lot of bad habits at college. Reading newspapers, making your own bed, clipping your nose hairs, eating peanut butter on vanilla ice cream. You'll see.

ZAN *(aside):* He's using *sentences* with me. He must've used 10 sentences already—nouns, verbs, adjectives. Everything! And not one of 'em ended with "zit breath" or "you little dip—"

BEN: Pass the cereal, please, Zanny. *(She hands him the cereal and milk with a look humans must have first given Vulcans.)* Thanks. *(He pours and eats. ZAN watches.)*

ZAN: Equal?

BEN: No thanks. *(She watches him eat. She gets an idea. She starts shoveling cereal in her mouth and eating loud. Really smacking away. Louder than Uncle Willie when he has his hearing aid turned off. No reaction from BEN.)*

ZAN: Aren't you gonna waste me?

BEN: What?

ZAN: Aren't you gonna punch my lights out? Bang, zoom, to the moon?

BEN: Zan, what're you talking about?

ZAN: I'm smacking my Alpha Bits. I've been sitting here smacking like I've got this massive chunk of Bubblicious in my mouth.

BEN: Yeah?

ZAN: You hate it when I smack my food! You used to sit there and just wait for the first smack so you could freak and stuff Crunchberries up my nose!

BEN *(laughs):* Sorry. I didn't hear you smacking. *(ZAN stands. She's losing her mind. She exits.)* Little Sis, could you bring me the orange juice. I left it in there like a geek. *(After a moment, she comes back in with a carton of orange juice, clutching six cartons of cereal. She sits and builds a cereal fortress around her bowl. She disappears behind. A beat. She begins humming. Louder. She peeks over at BEN. He's reading. She pops back down.)*

BEN: Hey, Zanny. It says here that U2's new album is going to be coming out . . . *(Notices the boxes)* Zanny? *(ZAN slowly raises her head above the cardboard wall.)* What're you doing?

ZAN: The cardboard wall. Oh, c'mon, Ben! You always wanted to kill me when I hogged all the cereal boxes. You didn't have anything to read. It used t'drive you outta your—

BEN: I've got something to read. *(Puts the paper down)* Oh . . . I'm being massively rude. Here I've been away for six months and I'm sitting here reading the paper like a full-on nimrod while you're hiding behind the Count Chocula. I'm sorry. How's school going?

ZAN *(knocks down the boxes)*: OK, OK. Who are you?!

BEN: Ben. I'm your brother Ben. I've only been away at school for six months. You didn't forget about—? (ZAN *stands, wild-eyed and breathing heavily. She's losing it. She dashes out.*) Zan? Zan, are you OK? Zan? Am I making you feel undervalued? Look, I'm sorry I was reading instead of—

(ZAN *bustles back in with an armful of stuffed animals.*)

ZAN: OK, if you're really Ben. My brother Ben. My big brother Ben who thinks I'm scuzzier than toe jam and lamer than Lionel Ritchie, then you won't be able to resist this. *(She flings a teddy bear at him.)* All right. OK. Twist the head off Pookey.

BEN: Why would I want to hurt Pookey? He's your favorite—

ZAN *(screams and tosses animals at him)*: Pull out their eyes. Punch in their noses. Drop kick 'em into the toilet. Pull their little toenails off. Make 'em do spins that'd make Michael Jackson sweat.

BEN: Why?

ZAN: C'mon! Knock it off, you dork! You've been home two days and you haven't mutilated one'a my animals. You used to string 'em up in my closet so I'd find 'em in the middle'a the night! You used to love to watch me scream when you stapled their little lips to the ceiling.

BEN *(laughing)*: Oh, yeah! That's right. I forgot about—

ZAN *(freaking)*: Oh, yeah! That's RIGHT! YOU FORGOT ABOUT! That's it, buddy!

BEN: What?

ZAN: That's IT, PAL! THAT'S IT! *(She pounces on him, poking, prodding, looking through his hair, and pulling back his eyelids.)*

BEN: Ow! Get off me, Zanny! What's going on!

ZAN: What have you done with my brother!

BEN *(laughing)*: Zanny, get off me!

ZAN: Who are you! Where is he! You . . . you're a pod people! You're a droid! A cyborg! You're a Stepford brother! The transporter beams got crossed on the Enterprise and MR. ROGERS' SOUL GOT STUCK IN MY BROTHER'S BODY!!

BEN: C'mon! Stop!

ZAN: Give me back my brother! Give him back! This one is way spaced! I don't know how to talk to a brother who doesn't begin sentences with "Yo, Spacklehead!" *(She is showing signs of slowing down.)*

BEN: Ah . . . you about through?

ZAN: Uh-huh. *(She sits.)*

BEN: You wanna tell me what's going on?

ZAN: Look, I don't know who you are, but you are not the big brother who used to sit on me and hang spit over my face.

BEN: You're right—

ZAN: Or who hid my Care Bears underwear in my organizer notebook so I'd discover 'em in the middle of math class.

BEN: I know I—

ZAN: OR who Krazy-Glued my toes together when he found out I wanted to take swimming lessons so I would have fins.

BEN: All right! I know! Sir, yes, sir! Guilty party present and accounted for, sir!

ZAN: All right. So who are you?

BEN *(leaning in close)*: All I can say is: I'm not your brother.

ZAN *(equally close)*: Are you my sister?

BEN: This is serious! Man, I was hoping I never had to tell anybody this. I was hoping nobody would notice the changes in me and I could go on living like a normal person. Like I was. But you saw through it, didn't you, Zanny?

ZAN: Am I gonna have to put on my boots?

BEN: It was terrifying, Sis. But I have to tell someone. I woke up one morning a couple of months ago. I was up early to get ready for a midterm. That's when I saw 'em. Little red marks on my arms. All over.

ZAN: What. Elf hickies?

BEN: No. Small, Zan. Little. Way weird. I tried to think of what might'a happened. Then it came to me.

ZAN *(cautiously intrigued)*: What?

BEN: Them. They did it.

ZAN: Them?

BEN: I never saw their faces. Just the lights from the machines they were working. It was like I was sleepwalking. Hypnotized. They led me into their ship.
Wow, I've never told anyone this stuff—they hooked me up to their . . .
gizmos.

ZAN: Get out.

BEN: They spoke in a strange tongue. It was English most'a the time. *(Strange
voice)* "How come you're such a bweenod?" they said.

ZAN: A "bweenod"?

BEN: It means "jerk."

ZAN: Of course.

BEN *(voice):* "Why you so mad all the time, bweenod?" Mad? I didn't think I was
mad. Scared spitless, maybe. I begged for them to take me back to my dorm.
But no go. Then they said, "See this light. It comes on when you're acting
like a bweenod." Well, it came right on and stayed on like a Christmas tree.
They shook their heads and clucked their . . . I don't know, tongues, I guess.
"Start treating everyone else the way you want to be treated, or . . ." then he
holds this big whoziwazzit over my head. "Or we gonna waste you with the
Dweezil Zapper." No, no, please! Not the Dweezil Zapper! Then one of them
threw me on the ground, sat on me, and hung spit. Then another stapled
my lips to the ceiling. Then I woke up back in bed. In my dorm. I thought
it was all a dream. But when I went to my midterm I found out one'a them
put a pair of my underwear in my bluebook.

ZAN: You're like, not trying to apologize to me for being a bweenod all these
years, are you?

BEN: You don't believe my story?

ZAN: Oh, I believe the part about your underwear in the bluebook. But I think
your dorky roommate, Herb, did that.

BEN: Herb's not smart enough to be that mean.

ZAN: I don't think the Klingon kidnap story's gonna go over big in church when
the pastor asks you to give your testimony on Incredible Big Brother Sunday. *(Pause)*

BEN: I missed you, Zanny. That's the truth. It hit me one day in Philosophy class.
What if I had a heart attack in the middle of a final or something and all
Zan'd remember about me is how I used to tickle her until she wet her
pants.

ZAN: Yeah. I'll be neurotic for life now, knucklehead. *(Pause)*

BEN: I'm really sorry. You were there, Zan. I'd get mad, and you were there. It was easy, you know. Someone'd make fun'a me; I'd make fun'a you. That's no excuse, I know. *(Pause)* I wanna start over, Zan. That's what I wanna do. Is that OK with you?

ZAN: Well. I wouldn't want to see you wailed on by the Dweezil Zapper.

BEN: I need to know I'm OK with you, huh? All right? Like I . . . didn't do any permanent damage.

ZAN: Naw, my toes came unstuck last month—

BEN: Zan!

ZAN: OK, OK! It's OK. I'd like to . . . start over. I mean, I always did kind'a like you. You weren't a nimrod all the time.

BEN: Thanks.

ZAN: But this doesn't mean you're, like, gonna kiss me in public, or tell all my boyfriends how sweet I am, and send me birthday cards with all the gooshy words underlined and lots of X's and O's by your name, does it?

BEN: Maybe. But not now, huh? We'll start out slow, OK. Take this brother-sister thing nice and easy. Sound all right?

ZAN: OK.

BEN: Good. *(Pause)* Yo, Spacklehead. Pass the Cocoa Puffs.

(ZAN *breaks out laughing and starts throwing cereal boxes at* BEN. *The lights go to:)*

(Blackout. Organ music begins to play.)

SKETCH 5

Stand Up, Stand Up for Jesus

CLASSROOM TEENAGERS
BILL TIBERT
MIKE
RACHEL   all junior-high- and/or high-school-age
GUY 1
GUY 2
TEACHER VOICE (offstage)
SCENE: a classroom

(The lights reveal a dozen or so TEENAGERS *sitting in a classroom. A chalkboard reads "Great American Literature." The students are bored, listening, whispering among themselves, doodling in their books, or sleeping. Some are giving a cursory listen to the unseen teacher—except for* BILL TIBERT, *who is shifting uneasily in his seat. He listens intently and looks around to see if anyone else is hearing what he is. He shakes his head.*

(We hear the offstage TEACHER VOICE *represented by either the squawky muted-horn sound of "Charlie Brown" fame, or as a dronish "Blah, blah, blabba, blah, blah, blah."* BILL *is outraged. He starts to raise his hand, looks around, then lowers it. He is very anxious. Wipes his hands on his pant legs. Deep breath. Finally, he can't take it anymore. He shoots a hand up. He leans forward to be noticed. He uses the other hand to support his upraised arm. Finally, he clears his throat.*

(The TEACHER VOICE *stops.)*

BILL *(quietly)*: Ah . . . I don't think you're telling the truth.

(The TEACHER VOICE *continues, ignoring* BILL. BILL *looks around, amazed. Some of the students are paying a bit more attention.)*

BILL: Ah, excuse me. Mr. Landers, I said I . . . *(The* VOICE *continues.* BILL *stands.)* I said, I don't think you're telling the truth. *(The* VOICE *stops. All eyes are on* BILL. *He looks around, uncomfortably.)* I . . . I believe that's just . . . your opinion. Ah . . . no, I just . . . really feel like I want to say something here. What you're saying is something you believe, it's not necessarily . . . *(he hears the rest of the class giggling or making exasperated noises)* . . . the truth.

MIKE: Siddown, Tibert! You geek!

BILL *(turning around)*: Deal with it, Johnson. I had to listen to your oral report on the poetry of the Beastie Boys' lyrics. *(A couple more "Come on!" "Get a life!" "Sit down!" "How embarrassing!"* BILL *ignores them and turns back to the teacher.)*

BILL: No, I'm talking about Jesus Christ. *(The place drops to a whisper.)* No, I think I know how you stand on Jesus, Mr. Landers, I just don't think it's fair the

36

way you . . . like, talk about Him like He's some retard you heard about. But you're not the final word on Christianity. You're an English teacher.

RACHEL: You are so bizarre, Tibert. Just shut up.

BILL: Wait . . . you go to my church, Rachel. What is this? (TEACHER VOICE *goes* "*blah, blah, blah.*") I know you have to finish the chapter. I'm just asking you to have a little more respect for what I believe when the subject comes up. No, wait . . . I don't hear you joking about Moses or . . . what's'is name? . . . Mohammed, or, or . . . Shirley MacLaine! Only Jesus. I've sat here and listened to you, that's how I know.

(The class is getting restless now. A few don't partake, but most are talking to each other and laughing. MIKE *tosses a piece of paper that hits* BILL *on the back of the head.)*

BILL: Excuse me, but you just said that the Bible was the most dangerous, sexist book ever conceived. You said we could all thank Jesus for the censorship of art. And you've used phrases like "Resurrection myth" and "the dark, corruptive influence of Christianity" since the semester began!

(The TEACHER VOICE *goes "Blah, blah, blah!" with a little more urgency. The class cracks up.)*

BILL: Now, that's not fair. See, you're doing it again. You're trying to make me look stupid for a belief that's different from yours. I am not trying to turn this classroom into a church service! Looks like you're the one with the pulpit in here. ("*Blah, blah, blah, blabba, blah.*")

BILL: Look . . . no, I'm sorry I interrupted you. It's just . . . no, it's just that . . . to me, Jesus is not a word in some Emily Dickinson poem or something. He's my Lord. So don't expect me to shut up if you're gonna make fun of 'im.

*(*BILL *sits down. The bell rings. The students begin filing out of class, looking at* BILL *like he was from another planet.)*

RACHEL: Thanks a lot, dork.

*(*BILL *keeps his head down, writing in his notebook. Three guys walk up.* MIKE *is one of them. He shoves* BILL'*s pencil.* BILL *does nothing.* MIKE *exits. After a moment, he looks up. The two other guys are standing there. Pause.)*

GUY 1: Dude. *(He gives* BILL *a high five and goes out.)*

GUY 2: Killer.

*(*BILL *looks around. The room is empty. He picks up his books and goes out. The lights fade to:)*

(Blackout. The organ music begins again.)

ANNOUNCER: Well, it's another Friday night in Warmwater. Families are just settling in around the TV with their piping-hot bowls of Orville Redenbacher's. Pastor Dorcas, with his mug of steaming hot cocoa, is putting the finishing touches on Sunday's sermon, "Jesus, the Parking Lot Project, and You." Mayor and Mrs. Stoker are preparing for another evening of "Falcon Crest," "Dallas," and "The Old-Fashioned Gospel Hour." And the teenagers of Warmwater, those blessed paragons of sweet spirituality, are spending the evening in the pursuit of godly and wholesome activities to fill the time until their 11 P.M. curfews.

GIRL'S VOICE *(off)*: Mark, I told you to knock it off!

ANNOUNCER: Well, most of them, anyway.

SKETCH 6

The Sex Police

MARK: high-school-age guy
BRITTANY: high-school-age girl
OFFICER 1: high-school-age guy/girl
OFFICER 2: high-school-age guy/girl
SCENE: a front room

(In the darkness we hear BRITTANY's voice, irritated and a little afraid, and MARK's voice cajoling.)

BRITTANY: Come on . . . stop!

MARK: What is your problem?

(The lights suddenly crash on.)

MARK: Hey, what is this?!

(MARK and BRITTANY are sitting on the couch. He's trying to put his arms around her. She's slightly pushed back and has both hands wrapped around his wrists, restraining him.)

MARK: Who's there? What's going on?!

(Suddenly OFFICER 1 and OFFICER 2 pop up from behind the sofa. They are dressed in blue uniforms, caps, gloves, and badges.)

OFFICERS: The Sex Police!

OFFICER 1: Hold it right there, buddy.

MARK: What are you—?

OFFICER 2 *(coming around and showing ID; Dan Ackroyd delivery):* We're the Sex Police, mister.

OFFICER 1: Don't make a move.

BRITTANY: Too late. He already did.

MARK: Is this some kind'a joke?

OFFICER 1: Do we look funny?

MARK: Well, I—

OFFICER 2: No, this is a nightmare, pal. And you're about to wake up. Now on your feet. Move away from her. Back up. Come on.

BRITTANY: Yeah, move back, pal.

OFFICER 1: Up against the wall.

MARK *(does so):* Wait a minute. Did her parents send you over here? *(To* BRITTANY) Did you tell your parents I—?

OFFICER 2 *(calling off):* All right, bring in the hose!

MARK *(wide-eyed):* The WHAT!

OFFICER 1: Cold water. That ought'a bring you back to room temperature.

BRITTANY: Yeah! *(She stands.)* Hose him down! Soak him to his Reeboks! Oh, no. He doesn't like cold showers, does he? I must'a told him to take a MILLION of 'em!

MARK: Britt! Babe! *(Goes to her)* Don't let them just—

OFFICER 1: Whoa! The perp's movin'! (OFFICER 2 *secures* MARK *with handcuffs and moves him away.)*

MARK: I thought you told me your parents didn't know I was coming over here tonight!

OFFICER 2: Uh-oh. Sounds like we've got a conspiracy going on here.

BRITTANY: Get out. I didn't tell my parents anything. *(To* OFFICER) He knows they go bowling on Saturday nights.

OFFICER 1: Uh-huh. *(Off)* OK, bring in the hose!

MARK: No water! NO WATER! I'm . . . fine.

OFFICER 1: I don't know. Check his temp, Officer.

OFFICER 2 (*shining a flashlight in his eyes*): He's cooling down. (*Looks down his throat. Checks his pulse.*) He's a bit sweaty, though. (*Wipes hand*)

OFFICER 1: Good. Name?

MARK: Mark Davidson. Sorry I don't have a rank or serial number to give you.

OFFICER 2: Oh, we got Mr. Guffaw here, don't we.

OFFICER 1: Age?

BRITTANY: Five.

MARK: Nuh-uh!

BRITTANY: Then how come you throw tantrums every time anyone tells you no.

MARK: Lay off. I'm 16.

OFFICER 1: Nationality?

MARK: I'm American.

OFFICER 2: Oh, not Italian?

MARK: No.

OFFICER 2: Then how come ya got roamin' hands, bub!

MARK: Yuk, yuk. Just whadd'ya want with me anyways?

OFFICER 1: Mark Davidson, 16, we're placing you under arrest for being a Class A jerk, for lying, and for illegal use of hands.

MARK: I'm not a . . . , ah, I never laid a hand . . . ah, when did I lie?!

OFFICER 1: Did you or did you not tell . . . (*checks paper*) . . . Brittany . . . that it was her fault that you got all . . . (*embarrassed*) . . . well, you know. I can't even say it out loud. (*He goes to* MARK *and whispers in his ear.*)

MARK: I said that?!

OFFICER 2: Sounds pretty stupid with all the lights on, don't it?

BRITTANY: You mean, that was a lie! It wasn't my fault he got all—?

MARK: Babe—

OFFICER 1: You're also being detained for various and assundried really stupid and very, very old lines that have been deemed a crime against intelligence. (*Deadpan delivery*) "Oh, baby, baby, come on if you love me."

OFFICER 2: "Don't you know you make me feel this way?"

OFFICER 1: "Honey, don't be a tease."

OFFICER 2: And the ever popular, "What's the matter, baby, are you . . . scared?"

BRITTANY (stunned): He did say that to me!

OFFICER 1: Officer, read him his rights.

OFFICER 2: You have the right to remain ashamed of yourself. Anything you have done can and will come back to you in the court of life. You have the right to make an apology. If you do not want to make an apology, you're really a jerk. You have the right to make one phone call, and it had better be to your youth pastor.

MARK: I'm sorry. It was, like, the heat of the moment, OK. Come on, hey, I'm just a guy.

BRITTANY: It's the heat of every moment, Mark.

MARK: I like you. I like you a lot. Is that a crime?

BRITTANY: If you liked me so much, then why didn't you stop pushing when I told you I didn't want to do anything more? Did you think I was kidding?

MARK: Hey, Britt, we've been going out three weeks already.

OFFICER 2: Wow, you're practically married.

OFFICER 1: All right, pal, who put you up to this?

MARK: What?

OFFICER 1: Come on, you didn't invent those lines by yourself. You were coached. Set up. Who lied to you first? It'll go easier on ya, kid.

MARK: You guys want me to fink?!

OFFICER 2: Yeah.

MARK: OK. (He thinks.) "Don't be a tease." I got that from my dad. He told me all women are teases. It's their nature.

BRITTANY: Your dad told you that?

OFFICER 1 (writing and shaking his head): Dad. Who else?

MARK: My big brother told me if a girl liked you, she'd better show you. He told me all the babes can't wait to be with him. You must've arrested my brother. Phil Davidson?

OFFICER 2: Never heard of 'im.

MARK (crestfallen): Oh. The rest of the ideas I got from my friends, the movies, TV, graffiti, some magazines, and a George Michael album. Hey, you're not going to arrest my dad, are you?

OFFICER 1: We oughta. Take 'im away. (They start to move off.)

MARK: Brittany! Come on, help me!

BRITTANY: Wait. *(They stop.)*

OFFICER 2: Don't you want to press charges? *(Pause)*

BRITTANY: I guess not.

MARK: Whoa. Thanks.

BRITTANY: On conditions.

MARK: Conditions?

OFFICER 1: OK. Fire.

BRITTANY: Tell him . . . Tell him I like him too, and when I kissed him I was only giving him affection, not an invitation to a good time.

OFFICER 1: She said, "Tell him I like him too—"

MARK: I heard her.

BRITTANY: And, contrary to popular opinion, it is not my responsibility to say no all the time. It's his responsibility too. I'm tired of being the sex police.

MARK: OK.

BRITTANY: And if he says, "Hey, I'm just a guy" one more time, I get to take him out back and shoot him.

OFFICER 2: Fair enough.

(MARK *is released. The* OFFICERS *move to the door.)*

OFFICER 1 *(to* BRITTANY*):* Just remember this. He didn't know you meant no, when you said no, you know? Now that he knows you know he knows you mean no, he oughta know better. You know?

BRITTANY *(confused):* No.

MARK: I know.

OFFICER 1: Good. *(To* MARK*)* And now that you know you can just say no. And she knows you know it. You'd better not say yes. Oh, and yes, no does not mean yes, know what I mean?

MARK/BRITTANY: Yes.

OFFICER 2: Good. *(To the audience)* And remember, the Sex Police are around every corner—

OFFICER 1: And behind every sofa.

OFFICERS: So, don't make us . . . *(they clap once)* . . . slap a restraining order on you. *(They go out.* MARK *and* BRITTANY *look at each other. They smile. They sit on the couch. After a moment,* MARK *puts his arm around* BRITTANY. *Pause. They both fire a quick glance behind the sofa. The lights fade to:)*

(Blackout.)

ANNOUNCER: We shall return to clean-cut, caring, carnal Warmwater in just a moment. But first, another word from our sponsor.

SKETCH 7

Testimony Power for Good Kids: A Commercial

YOUTH GROUP TEENS
SPEAKER: a high-school- or college-age guy/girl
PITCHMAN: high-school-age guy
SCENE: youth group room

(Lights. A youth group is sitting on the floor around the SPEAKER, *who is about 18. Most of them are nodding off, doodling, or staring into space, bored to tears. The* SPEAKER *fumbles nervously with 3" x 5" cards, looking up every few moments to see the crowd's reactions. The* SPEAKER *is near panic.)*

SPEAKER: Wheew . . . boy, oh, boy. It was a real downhill spiral for me then. I was . . . well, y'know . . . I, ah, I faked being sick! Just so I could stay home from school! *(Someone yawns)* I . . . I got a C in algebra! Then . . . then . . . then in my senior year I went radical, y'know? I . . . turned my back on God! Well, I skipped youth group for a whole month anyways. And I was drinkin' big time! Beer at parties! Well, a couple of beers . . . ah, yeah, well, just one beer at these parties—OK! One party! One beer at this one party! But I was really blowin' it, lemme tell you! A major blow-it case! Honest!

(They freeze. Piano tremolo. The PITCHMAN *bounds in carrying a video and a cassette.)*

PITCHMAN: Ladies and gentlemen, how many of you have a testimony that sounds like this one?

SPEAKER: And so I started sayin' to myself, "Do you really want to go on with this wasted life?" Y'know, like, watchin' too much TV, sticking dishsoap in the fountain downtown, walking against the streetlight! *(Someone snores. They all freeze.)*

PITCHMAN *(clicking his tongue):* Pathetic, really. Just look at these people! They're waiting to hear something dramatic! Something truly inspiring!

43

SPEAKER (*throwing up the cards*): OK! OK! I'M A GOOD KID! I'M SORRY! I love God . . . I love my parents. I really wanted to be a heathen. Deep down. Honest! I just always had too much homework. (*They freeze.*)

PITCHMAN: Do you find yourself with a less than stirring faith journey? Have you always been the kid parents pointed to and said . . . (*mimes smacking a child on the back of the head*) . . . "Why can't you be more like him, toad head!" Do you get a knot in your stomach every time the youth pastor asks you to give your testimony because you know the closest you ever got to being a pagan was pretending you were smoking on frosty mornings walking to school?

SPEAKER: I did that!

ALL: SIDDOWN! (*The* SPEAKER *sits.*)

PITCHMAN: Being a good kid is wonderful. Really. I mean, it must have taken a lot of discipline to keep your nose out of all that sin. And I'm sure mom and dad appreciated it. But now you have others to think about. What about the youth group? Don't you think you owe them something to shout "amen" about? (*Shows a video box.*) Well now you can with "Testimony Power: 30 Minutes to the Sinner You Always Wanted to Be!" from Nerdman Videos.

Now you can turn that scary Brady Bunch background into a testimony you and your family can be proud of. Yes, "Testimony Power" is for you. First, you'll get to see and hear the conversion stories of rock stars, celebrities, and sports legends. Just everyday folk to inspire and encourage you. Next, a famous public speaker will take you step by step through your new, reconstructed testimony. He'll cover such topics as "Don't Be Afraid to Be Vague," "The Power of Tears," and my personal favorite, "Backsliding: Your Second Chance at a Dynamic Conversion!" (*Suddenly the others spring to life. The* SPEAKER *is now a renewed and fiery preacher.*)

SPEAKER: God was deeealing with me. Yes, He was! But it was to get worse! (*They lean forward, all ears.*) I was lyin' to my parents! Messin' up in school! How many of you know what I'm talkin' about! (*Hands shoot up all over.*) And then there were the parties. The parties! Do I have to say more? (*They shake their heads.*) Lyin', dissipation—even vandalism! I was rotten, people. ROTTEN TO THE CORE! (*They burst into applause.*)

PITCHMAN (*clapping and shaking his head*): Oh, just listen to him go! It's a miracle, isn't it? And to think, just a short time ago he was just a kid who loved Jesus because Jesus first loved him. So, don't let an untainted past keep you from dynamic spirituality. Get "Testimony Power" today! Send your check for $39.99 to—

SPEAKER: Spewed Associations, people! Fourteen Forty-two Complacent Corners! Uh-huh! Warmwater, Illinois! Six-oh, six-oh, nine!

PITCHMAN: That's right. Show them God is really working in your life!

(Blackout.)

ANNOUNCER: Yes, the school year is winding on here in perky, peachy, pitiful Warmwater. The holidays are well over, and the young people have settled into their second semesters with keen determination and the utmost discipline. And don't think this kind of steely, gung-ho, go-gettum attitude doesn't spill over into their desire to fulfill the Great Commission! Why, even now, one youth group is smack-dab in the middle of an evangelism campaign. And they're taking it very seriously. Let's take a peek, shall we?

SKETCH 8

The Great Nail-the-Pagan Evangelistic Campaign

YOUTH GROUP TEENS
TIM
RALPH
JUDY   all junior-high- and/or high-school-age
ELAINE
CAROLINE
SCENE: youth group room

(Lights come up in a youth group room. Chairs and songbooks are scattered throughout. A banner on the wall reads "NAIL-THE-PAGAN CAMPAIGN HEADQUARTERS" and "BODY COUNTS FOR JESUS!" The young people are all standing at attention. TIM DOWN, in fatigues and a combat helmet, is addressing the troops.)

TIM: At ease, soldiers. *(The young people relax.)* Now, I know it's hard out there, men . . . and women . . . ah, girls. People! Yes, I know it's a war out there, people! And you're drawin' fire from every quarter. We're in what I call "The War of the World." But I need you all to knuckle down in the trenches and get us the bodies! Attendance is low, as you can see. And it's up to you to fill these chairs, do you read me! I'm tired'a makin' excuses for you to the youth pastor! Do I make myself perfectly clear?!

YOUNG PEOPLE: Sir, yes, sir!

TIM *(in his face)*: Private Ralph!

RALPH: Sir, yes, sir!

TIM: Details, soldier. War stories. Let's have it.

RALPH: I drew major combat this week, General Tim. I took homeroom on Tuesday single-handed. I laid down a cover fire of "If You Were to Die Tonight" tracts and took 'em out with the "Way Living Bible, Dude" New Testaments.

TIM: Bodies, soldier?

RALPH: Nailed four pagans, sir! Crossed over to our side.

TIM: Where are they, son?

RALPH: You wanted me to invite 'em to church?

TIM: Of course, soldier! Otherwise, you have no proof of the hits!

RALPH: I'll go back and recon, sir. I just don't remember who they were.

TIM: Well, we'll list 'em as missing in action. Private Judy!

JUDY (snapping to): Present, sir! I . . . I made an aerial attack on Friday, sir!

TIM: Details, soldier!

JUDY: I threw John 3:16 stickers into the quad from the roof of the science lab during lunchtime.

TIM: Ingenious, soldier! Body count?

JUDY: Well . . . some of the enemy picked the stickers up, sir.

TIM: Body count! WE NEED A BODY COUNT! That's what evangelism is all about, people! Nail 'em and bring 'em in!

(ELAINE is throwing up her hand, urgently.)

TIM: I like your spunk, Private Elaine! Talk to me, soldier!

ELAINE: I bagged eight pagans, sir! Nailed 'em before they walked into their SAT test last Saturday. All of 'em said they believed in God and Jesus and stuff. They were even shaking with joy.

TIM: Excellent, soldier! Get them with their defenses down. OK, give me the names.

ELAINE: Names, sir?

TIM: Names, soldier!

ELAINE: Oh, I didn't get their names, ranks, or serial numbers.

TIM: What's wrong with you people! How are we gonna know if we're winning if you don't get these people into our camp! Private Caroline, report!

CAROLINE: Sir, yes, sir! Ah . . . last week I got a chance to have a long talk with Lauren Jackson in study hall.

TIM (checks list): Lauren Jackson? Lauren Jackson! You've been pursuing this particular enemy ever since the campaign began, soldier!

CAROLINE: Begging the general's pardon, but she's not the enemy any more, sir. She's my friend now. This week she told me all about her parents' divorce. It was real hard for her to talk about. We cried together.

TIM: Verrrrry touching, soldier. Yes, indeed. NOW NAIL HER! We are not here, I repeat, not here to fraternize with the enemy! I want her here next week, got that, soldier? I want to see that seat filled, do I make myself clear? AT-TENTION! *(They all snap to.)* All right, puppies! No more Mr. Nice Guy. I want it to look like Pentecost in here next Wednesday night. Operation Pentecost! Remember, the enemy is wily. They will attempt to become your friends. Do not allow this to happen, people. If they offer information on their lives, take it and use it. But do not be taken in by their needs! Now get out there and kick souls and take names! Move it, move it, MOVE IT! COM-PAAAAANY . . . DIIIIISMISSED!

(Blackout. Organ music.)

ANNOUNCER: Mimi Von Schnookums. That name strikes hunger in the stomachs of more than one youngster in Warmwater! Mimi is known for her gift of hospitality—and for her, shall we say, sugar thumb? The kids all sure love Mimi. Particularly her . . . killer brownies. Let's drop in on yet another youth group party at the Schnookumses.

SKETCH 9

Brownie Points

YOUTH GROUP TEENS (onstage actors or voices on tape)
KEVIN
TIFFANY   all junior-high- and/or high-school-age
PAIGE
SCENE: Mimi Von Schnookums' front room

(In the darkness we hear party sounds—people talking, laughing, and eating. A spot comes up on a buffet table, center stage. It is covered with incredible eats—and a huge plate of brownies right in the middle. The spot widens and we see KEVIN, TIFFANY, and PAIGE. They are staring at the table, moving to different positions to look at it. After a moment, they slowly begin to circle the table, oblivious to anyone else, including each other. Occasionally they might walk into other party guests, but they take no notice. Even though all three are obsessed with the food, they are very normal-looking teenagers in body size. After a moment, they stop and look out at the audience.)

KEVIN/TIFFANY/PAIGE: Mimi Von Schnookums' triple-fudge, three-layered, chocolate-frosted brownies look outrageous, don't they? *(Small pause)* WHY DID I HAVE TO COME TO THIS STUPID PARTY?!

(They go back to circling. KEVIN steps out to address the audience, while the others continue their march.)

KEVIN: I'd give anything to have one'a those radical brownies. I'd snag the whole plate, if I could. Two points! Takedown! But I gotta make weight tomorrow for the match. I gotta. Alls I been eatin' the whole week is cottonballs, lemon water, and All Bran. It's way bizarre. If I'm not in class, I'm in the bathroom. I'm starving. I asked my coach if I could just go ahead and wrestle 145s instead'a 138s. It'd be a lot easier on me. *(Shouts)* "What's the matter, Benson, you can't make weight? Scarfin' up too many Ding-Dongs at lunchtime? Show me a little self-control, willya!" I felt like Lord Major General Wimposaurus of the Universe. What can I do? Have you ever not made weight? Standing there praying it doesn't tip. And if it does . . . look out. It's the worst. You feel like you just . . . let down the whole world. And then I'd have to tell my dad. Dead meat. Coach is right, man. I'm such a wimp. After this party, I'll turn up the heat in the basement, put on my sweats, and do laps all night. My mom'll lecture me on my health, but my dad'll think I'm tough. I'll just do what it takes to make 138 tomorrow. Whatever it takes.

KEVIN/TIFFANY/PAIGE: And so I shouldn't eat anything. Not even a brownie. *(KEVIN joins the circle. TIFFANY steps out.)*

TIFFANY: Everyone looks on a fat person's plate to see what they're eating. You know it's true. Look at 'em all. They're just watchin' me to see if the hippo goes straight for the mud. Well, I'm not gonna do it. *(Laughs)* Yeah, well my

48

mom says I'm just big-boned. "If you lose too much weight you'll look stupid. C'mon, honey, have some more tuna casserole." So what do I look like to people? Big-boned? Get out. The word is fat. Lose *pudgy, overweight, heavy, plump.* The word is F-A-T. Gi-huge-ic. You won't catch me near that table. I touch anything over there and it might as well have an arrow on it that points straight to my rear. And if I do blow it, it's back on aspirins and Diet Coke to lose it. And I can do that for almost a week without getting too wasted. Oh, you don't think I can? You don't think I have any willpower, is that it? Well, you can just stare all you want.

KEVIN/TIFFANY/PAIGE: And so I can't eat anything. Not even a brownie. *(She steps back into the circle.* PAIGE *steps out.)*

PAIGE: I am huge! I'm an asteroid! Look at me. Every time I move I can feel it jiggling. And it's totally my fault. My whole family looks like they stepped right out of a commercial for Yoplait. It's my metabolism. I'm the one that gets stuck with the metabolism of a slug. My mom eats all this lo-cal stuff. She's a vegetarian. She won the Boney Maroni Lifetime Achievement Award. I can't eat a thing. It shows up on me somewhere in minutes. I gained three pounds in one day. It's true. I tested it one time. I weighed myself first thing in the morning. Then I ate normally all day. And I weighed myself before I went to bed. I had to adust the scale back to zero. My mom is so paranoid she has it set at negative two pounds and we all pretend not to notice. Anyway, I gained three pounds! I even subtracted one pound because I figured the Jack-in-the-Box fajita wasn't digested yet. Still three pounds! In one day! I got so mad. I screamed! "It's not my fault! It's my metabolism!" Then I said, "That's no excuse. It is my fault. It's all my fault. I'm such a pig. I have to control it, that's all." I could feel that stupid fajita just sitting there in my stomach, reminding me of what an idiot I am. So I locked the bathroom door and turned on the shower so nobody could hear me. I took control. At first it was hard. But now I know just where to put my finger so it's all gone. *(She snaps.)* Just like that. *(Small pause)* But I read somewhere that it's supposed to be bad for you. So, I try not to do it too often.

KEVIN/TIFFANY/PAIGE: And so I won't eat anything. Not even a brownie. *(She steps back. All three are circling now.* PAIGE *sees* KEVIN.)*

PAIGE: Hey, Kevin. How's the season going for you?

KEVIN: I'm doing all right. *(Looks off)* Hey, Mark.

PAIGE: Pretty good party, huh? At least the food looks incredible. Did you see Schnookums' brownies?

KEVIN: How could you miss 'em? She's brutal with the chocolate. Maybe that's why her kids are all blimpozoids.

PAIGE: Yeah . . . huge. (*Changes subject*) You guys sure are lucky, you know that? Especially you sportos. You get to eat anything you want. Always working out.

KEVIN: We still have to watch it a little sometimes. Have to make weight. I'm startin' to pork out.

PAIGE: Come on! It's a breeze, huh? Guys' metabolisms are different. They burn calories up so fast. You don't have to work so hard.

KEVIN: I s'pose. (*Off*) Yo, Tiffany! Well, see ya 'round, Paige.

PAIGE (*a little hurt*): Sure.

(*They start to circle.* KEVIN *spots* TIFFANY. *It's obvious he's attracted to her.*)

KEVIN: Tiffany. How ya doin'?

TIFFANY: Ah, Kevin, right?

KEVIN: Dead on. From youth group . . . and school. I'm . . . ah, on the wrestling team.

TIFFANY: Yeah.

KEVIN: This table's wild, isn't it?

TIFFANY: Killer.

KEVIN: You check out the brownies over there?

TIFFANY: Oh? Where?

KEVIN: In the middle. The ones that're the size'a Lake Michigan.

TIFFANY: You know, I didn't even notice 'em. I've been eating those vegetables over there all night.

KEVIN: You want me to get you one? A brownie, I mean.

TIFFANY: Oh, no thanks. One'a those'd waste my diet.

KEVIN: Really? (*Looks at her*) Yeah, you have lost some weight, haven't you.

TIFFANY (*shaken*): A . . . yeah, a little, I guess. (*She moves off.*)

KEVIN (*after her*): I mean, you look great. (*Stops*) What a jerk. I can't even control my mouth. (*They continue on.* TIFFANY *runs into* PAIGE.)

TIFFANY: Hi, Paige.

PAIGE: Oh, hi, Tiffany. I like your sweater.

TIFFANY: Thanks. The Gap. The hero of my wardrobe. (*Small pause*) Hey, how d'you do it, Paige? You been goin' to this church since forever and you manage to stay so thin in spite'a all these porkoid festivals.

PAIGE: Are you kidding? I'm a pig.

TIFFANY: You're what?! If you're a pig, I'm the state of Texas. Come on. You're whole family looks great. You guys eat tofu day and night, or what?

PAIGE: I don't know why you're complaining, Tiff. You could eat anything you wanted. You could . . . eat one of those brownies and it wouldn't show anywhere, except in your teeth.

TIFFANY: What? How do you think I got these hips?

PAIGE: You look great the way you are. Just the way you are. (*She walks away. They are in the circle again.*)

TIFFANY: The way I am? Big-boned is what she means. It'll never change. I deserve all the stares.

PAIGE: What does she know. Her mom doesn't look like Jane Fonda. Why am I even trying?

KEVIN: Coach is prob'ly right. I am a major wimp. No control.

(*They stop. They grab napkins and go straight for the brownies. They pick one up each and wrap it in the napkin, trying to hide it. They all see each other. There is a moment of tension, then they break and come downstage.*)

ALL: I'll just eat this one. (*Small pause*) I know how to get rid of it later.

(*Blackout.*)

(*In the darkness, the organ music begins to play, sweetly. After a moment, we hear a girl's voice saying, "Excuse me . . . ah, excuse me a minute . . ."*)

ANNOUNCER: Well, the school year is rapidly drawing to a close here in the shining buckle of God's Bible Belt.

VOICE: Can I have your attention . . . just one sec . . . ah . . .

ANNOUNCER: There have been hayrides, swim parties, singalongs, ski trips, video parties, progressive dinners, skate nights, canoe trips, and backpack Bible studies.

VOICE: If I could . . . this is real important . . . I just want to say that . . . ah, could I just interrupt . . .

ANNOUNCER: But there is one final youth group ritual that we have yet to see. It usually happens about this time of year. The weather turns sunny, the flowers are out in full bloom, the robins are flitting from tree to tree with pieces of nests in their graceful bills. And the young people of Warmwater find themselves strangely drawn to that one unavoidable activity.

YOUTH GROUP: NOT THE ALL-CHURCH CAR WASH?!

Workin' at the Car Wash Blues

YOUTH GROUP TEENS (offstage voices)
MUFFY
WESLEY
MARION
ANDREA
DAN
TEEN 1
TEEN 2
TEEN 3
TEEN 4
TEEN 5
TEEN 6
TEEN 7
TEEN 8
DOUGHNUT THROWERS (offstage)
SCENE: youth group room

(The sound of a loud, piercing, rally-size whistle. The lights come on. MUFFY STEWART is standing center with her whistler fingers in her mouth. She is a bit surprised by the sudden silence.)

MUFFY: Thank you. I just want to talk to you all for a minute. Oh, by the way. *(Giggles)* I'm Muffy Stewart. My dad's one of the deacons here and all that. Well, anyways, I'm one of the program planners—one of the Carpenter's Workbench. That's what we're called. Anyways, I wanted to tell you all about summer camp this year. We're going up to Mount Pamphylia this year, well, like we do every year, anyways, and this year we're planning . . . well, Pastor Dave and all of us, anyways, are planning some radical speakers and stuff. Plus all the other stuff, like food and beds and swimming and all. Anyways, the other problem is we have to pay for all this, y'know. For the speakers and the s'mores and for people who can't afford to go and stuff. OK, so we went over our budget and all. *(She reads from a ledger sheet of paper.)* And as close as we can figure, after Christian night at Rage-oid Water Mountain, we are . . . about . . . \$12,542 in the hole. *(She looks up.)* Well . . . Come on! We did a lotta stuff! All right, all right! We have an idea. Listen! We like worked it out and decided we needed a fund-raiser to help us out. We thought a lot about it and came up with a—

YOUTH GROUP *(off)*: YOUTH GROUP CAR WASH!

MUFFY: How'd you know? We just decided last night. Wesley, did you tell everyone before I even got up here? I'm so sure. Anyways, next weekend we're going to all meet at the church at 8 A.M. and wash cars all day in the parking lot. It'll be great! Bring buckets and sponges and rags. No short shorts, Regina. We'll provide doughnuts and drinks and stuff. It'll be outrageous! I've got tickets to sell, and we're announcing it at every service all week and stuff. We're gonna be swamped, and we really need your help. Please, please, puhleeeze! OK? I'll start the sign-up sheet with Marion. Thanks, you guys. Totally. Your help, like, means a whole lot to me.

(Blackout. In the darkness we hear loud horns honking. The lights come up on MUFFY, ANDREA, WESLEY, *and* MARION *who are all sitting in folding chairs or on the floor, dejected. There is a boom box, one bucket, a sponge, a roll of paper towels, and a half-used bottle of Windex. The door is wedged closed with a chair.)*

MUFFY *(stunned)*: Honestly, everybody put their names on the sign-up sheet, right? How could they all just not show up!

WESLEY: There must be 4,000 cars out there. All the deacons're here. I even saw Myrtle Fetschwanger and Pastor Dorcas. We're dead meat.

MARION: It's like half'a Warmwater was in four-wheelin' mud competition last night at Falwell Stadium. I never seen so much dirt in my life.

ANDREA: It's always just us. Every time there's work to do we roll outta bed and get down here and the rest've 'em sit in front of their TV's eating Chocolate Gagoid Puffs and watching "Teenage Mutant Ninja Turtles."

MUFFY: Now I know how my dad feels when no one shows up for deacon meetings. *(Loud horns)*

WESLEY: We're dead meat. I'll never live to see Wheaton College.

MARION: We got one bucket and one sponge!

MUFFY: We can do it! *(She stands.)* We'll just have to work twice as hard! Let's go! Let's go! Let's go!

ALL: Cool it, Muffy. *(She sits, pouting. There is a pounding at the door.* WESLEY *goes to it.)*

WESLEY: Who is it?

DAN *(off)*: It's Dan! Open it! Hurry up! *(*WESLEY *opens the door.* DAN *breaks into the room with an armful of doughnut boxes and trays of coffee.)* They don't want doughnuts anymore! I can't hold 'em off with jelly-filled! They're getting this glazed look in their eyes. Fetschwanger's already lost it. She's screamin' stuff like, "unreliable little twerps!" and runnin' over custard-filled long johns with her Pinto.

MUFFY *(jumping up)*: Let's get out the church directory and call the whole youth group. We'll rouse 'em up. We'll get 'em motivated. Let's go, let's go, let's go!

ALL: Sit down, Muffy. *(She sits, pouting again. Horns start to blare.* DAN *looks off.)*

DAN: Mrs. Fetschwanger! Please, put down the hose! *(Turns back)* She's got a hose. She's starting to wash cars with Biz and some Kleenex. *(Dashing off)*

Mrs. Fetschwanger! You don't have to do that! MRS. FETSCHWANGER! (WESLEY *barracades the door.*)

ANDREA: Well, we've gotta do something. Either we start washing cars or we tell 'em all to go home.

MUFFY: What about summer camp!

ANDREA: How do they expect anything to happen around here? Oh, they'll grab their suits for a swimming party, or marshmallows for campfire night, but ask 'em to pick up a sponge or a broom, or mail some fliers, and it's always the same five who do it. Well, I, for one, am massively burned out on the whole thing.

MARION: I say we blow this off, walk into youth group next Wednesday night, and tell 'em all that summer camp is history.

MUFFY: No, no, no . . . Think. Let's think. I mean, what do our parents do? Hardly anyone ever shows up for their planning meetings or work parties, either.

WESLEY/MARION/ANDREA: THEN THEY SHOULD CANCEL CHURCH! (*Horns blare incredibly loud. A knock at the door.*)

DAN (*off*): It's DAN! LET ME IN! LET ME IN! (WESLEY *opens the door. Doughnuts start flying in—along with angry voices, "Get out here!" "We've waited long enough!" "Lazy kids!" etc.* EIGHT TEENS *pile into the room, first, looking rather shaken up.* DAN *follows close behind, covering his head. His boxes have been torn to shreds. He has coffee stains on his shirt.* DAN *picks up a doughnut and throws it back.*) You shouldn't play with your food! (*He slams the door and wedges the chair back. Silence. The "core group" now stands and stares at the* EIGHT TEENS, *who look sheepishly back. They've got comic books, Slurpies, fast food, and skateboards. No sign of a bucket or a sponge anywhere.*)

DAN: I found 'em. Down at the 7-11 on the corner. When they saw me they started to run. But some of the cars from the church followed me to see if I was takin' off or somethin'. They surrounded all of these guys. So I brought 'em back here.

(*The core group is moving closer, they are outnumbered but too mad to care.*)

TEEN 1: Look, we were on our way down here, OK.

MUFFY: But, like, where are your buckets and sponges?

TEEN 3: Oh, well, we were comin' down here to tell you that we couldn't come.

MUFFY: Why did you do this to us? I saw your names on the summer camp sign-up. How did you think we were gonna raise the money? (*Silence*)

WESLEY: I say we send 'em back out there.

ANDREA: And lock the doors!

MARION *(headline):* "Teenagers Stoned by Day-Old Maple Bars."

WESLEY: Film at eleven.

ANDREA: Open the door for 'em, Dan! Throw 'em out there. *(They move on the* EIGHT TEENS, *who look scared.)*

MUFFY: Wait! Let 'em tell us why they didn't show up. *(Pause)*

DAN: All right, you heard the lady. You wanna go back out there? Huh? Mark, your mom is out there. She hit me in the head with a glazed twist. OK, talk. *(Silence)* OK, open the doors! *(He grabs the chair.)*

TEEN 1: Wait, wait! I figured you guys were s'posed to do all this!

ANDREA: Hold it, Dan. What did you say?

TEEN 1: You guys are the core group. Didn't you sign up or something? I thought you guys took care of it.

MARION: What about you?

TEEN 2: I can't do nothin'. I'm not good at nothin'. I always mess stuff up.

ANDREA: What about you?

TEEN 3: Nobody ever asked me to my face. I'm tired of sign-up sheets. I didn't know you guys needed me here.

WESLEY: What's your story?

TEEN 4: I don't even know you guys! I went to the 7-11 to get some milk for my mom, and these cars surrounded me!

MUFFY *(sweeping toward him):* Oh, hi! My name's Muffy. This is Dan, Marion, Wesley, and Andrea. We'd just love to have you come back on Wednesday night! Marion, get 'im a tract.

ANDREA: OK, you. Fast!

TEEN 5: Ah . . . ah . . . I'm really busy this year. I'm in band and stuff . . . and stuff.

ANDREA: Yeah, yeah. You?

TEEN 6: I did all the work last year. Nobody ever came. I'm burned out.

TEEN 7: And I haven't been at youth group in six months. Nobody ever noticed till now.

WESLEY: What about you?

TEEN 8: OK, I'm a freeloader. I'll admit it. I never helped before and I always went to camp. I figured you guys had all the help you needed. I mean, camp always happened, didn't it? *(Pause)*

ANDREA: Well, you're wrong. We need you. Every one of you, whether you think you're qualified or not.

WESLEY: You didn't elect us to do everything, y'know. We didn't run for office. We're here because we wanna be.

MARION: We're a body here. We can't function without you. This group doesn't mean anything unless everybody understands that.

MUFFY: Yeah. *(Small pause)*

EIGHT TEENS *(ashamed)*: We're sorry.

ANDREA *(sighs)*: OK, Dan. We can't make 'em stay. Open the door and let 'em go. (DAN *goes to open the door.)*

TEEN 1: Wait! Don't open that!

TEEN 5: Yeah, my mom's out there, and she's gotta bear claw with my name on it.

ANDREA: So . . . what're you guys gonna do? *(Pause. The* EIGHT TEENS *look at each other.)*

TEENS: OK. We'll stay.

MUFFY: Great, you guys! Phenomenal! Way outrageous! I knew you guys'd come through for us! Totally dudical!

TEEN 4 *(to 5)*: Do we have to work with her?

WESLEY: What're we gonna wash the cars with, huh? We only got one bucket.

TEEN 3: Ah . . . my mom runs the "Proverbs 31 Woman" Beauty Parlor. She's got lots of towels and stuff.

MUFFY: Phenomenal!

TEEN 2: My family buys stuff in bulk. We've got a ton of those pop-up sponges!

MUFFY: Radical!

TEEN 8: My dad owns a janitorial business. He's got lots of buckets!

MUFFY: Too outrageous!

TEEN 4: My dad's a dentist! *(Silence)*

MUFFY: That's . . . neat. Anyways, you guys go get the stuff, 'kay? And we'll start on the first cars with our bucket. Great, huh? Let's go! Let's go! Let's go!

DAN (*pulling the chair away from the door*): Doughnut shields up! Phasers set on stun! Energize! (*The door opens and doughnuts fly in. They all rush out the door, with a cheer.* ANDREA *and* WESLEY *are the last to go.*)

WESLEY: You know, sometimes I wonder what would have happened if Jesus had to pick apostles from our youth group.

ANDREA: Well, we wouldn't have a church here, that's for sure.

WESLEY: Whaddyou mean?

ANDREA: I seriously doubt any of 'em would've showed up for the Great Commission.

WESLEY: You are brutal. (*They go out. The lights start to dim.*)

MUFFY (*off*): Wait! (*The lights stop. She runs in, looks around, and sees the bucket. She grins.*) Those guys! (*She picks it up.*) Youth group. Ya gotta love 'em. (*Turns to the audience*) Ya just gotta! (*She runs out. The lights fade to:*)

(*Blackout.*)

YUKE AND THE KILLER WINDOW

*Six Contemporary Sketches and Monologues
Based on Scripture*

What would an Enscoe collection be without a few contemporizations of Scripture?

"Yuke and the Killer Window" is a collection of six short sketches and monologues based on biblical characters and events. They take both serious and humorous looks at some issues teenagers face in their Christian life—like friendship, perfectionism, anger, feeling alive in Christ, and putting God first. In each play we've tried to be as frank and honest as we can. No sense in pulling punches when you live in a world like ours.

For subjects and models we've chosen Eutychus (who?); Jairus' Daughter; David and Jonathan; Shadrach, Meshach, and Abednego: Joseph (the Old Testament one); and Rhoda. We think we've covered just about every teenager we could find in the Bible.

All the pieces were designed with a minimum amount of props and sets, so they can be done in informal settings. They cover the gambit of styles from serious testimony approach to broad humor. The settings range from a TV studio to a high school gym.

If you want to do them all as a cycle of issue plays, it will take you about an hour. Separately, they range from 8 to 12 minutes in length. Some will work better with a churched audience—however, we suggest that "Dead to the World," "In Deep," and "Idol Threats" can be used in a more evangelistic program.

It is our desire that young people—as well as adults—don't see their biblical counterparts in the faith as dim, dull, and distant memories or cartoon characters slapped on felt boards in Sunday School. They lived and blazed with the same issues, conflicts, questions, doubts, and strength of character as we. The only place where we differ is in culture. And that is the very reason we have placed these sketches in a modern setting.

To those who will use these plays in ministry to young people, our prayers and admiration go with you.

The Big Save

A Sketch on Friendship
1 Samuel 17—18:4

Running Time

9 minutes

Cast

TEAMMATES: five high school guys
JONATHAN: high-school-age guy
DAVID: high-school-age guy
SCENE: High school gym or playing field. Day.

Props

Uniforms (appropriate to the season—football, baseball, basketball, or wrestling. DAVID's uniform is way too big.)
Letter jacket
Sling

Production Notes

Friendship is marked by many elements, but one of its most salient and celebratory qualities is the ability for one friend to be able to rejoice over the successes and joys of the other. This quality was written all over the friendship of Jonathan and David—from the moment they met at Goliath's demise.

It takes a real understanding of God's unlimited source of blessing to guard against jealousy and bitterness in a friendship. This sketch taps into what has been called the "Zero-Sum" theory, the belief that if you are given something—say, a job in a field I'm trying to break into—then that means there's less available for me. As Christians, we know that what God has for us, He will not withhold if we ask—no matter what those around us have been given.

In "The Big Save" Jonathan is the self-assured, all-around jock who is a favorite in every high school circle. David is the new kid, a little socially inappropriate, but intense, earnest, and very talented. The Goliath victory is only alluded to in competition language.

(In the darkness we hear the sound of a crowd cheering. This shouldn't be a sound effects cut but a real group applauding, whistling, and shouting.

(A buzzer or bell sounds to tell us something is over.

(Lights. A group of TEAMMATES *[5] in uniforms are standing in the playing area, staring off at something or someone. These guys have major attitudes.* JONATHAN, *wearing a letter jacket and his arm in a sling, stands in the middle of them. It's obvious he's the leader of this group.)*

TEAMMATE 1: Get real. That was luck. Totally.

TEAMMATE 2: Yeah. Lucky shot.

TEAMMATE 3: He couldn't do that again in a million years.

TEAMMATE 4: Even if he wanted to.

TEAMMATE 5: Right place, right time.

JONATHAN: Don't you guys get it? He saved our tails.

TEAMMATE 1: Who is he, anyway? Came outta nowhere to do that.

TEAMMATE 2: Never seen 'im. Musta been sittin' on the bench all this time.

TEAMMATE 3: He's a total wimp. His uniform's too big for 'im!

TEAMMATE 4: Must be about 12!

TEAMMATE 5: I can't believe your dad let him out there to play.

JONATHAN: We were getting slaughtered out there. He won it for us. The dude's all right.

(At this, DAVID *walks in, breathless and sweating. He wears a uniform and shoes that are way too big for him. The* TEAMMATES *check him up and down.* DAVID *stands there, very uncomfortable.* JONATHAN *finally steps forward and holds up his hand.* DAVID *grins and slaps him a high five. Reluctantly and coolly, the others high-five* DAVID, *who really gets into it.)*

TEAMMATE 3: You were all right out there.

TEAMMATE 1: Workin'.

TEAMMATE 5: Don't let it go to your head, wimpozoid. *(The* TEAMMATES *walk off.)*

DAVID *(calling after them)*: Great. Yeah. Thanks. Thanks, you guys. *(He's left alone onstage with* JONATHAN. *Long pause.)*

JONATHAN: Thanks. You saved us out there. We were lookin' pretty bad. Those guys were killin' us. Especially that front guy. That . . . Godzilla-looking guy. *(Laughs)* You sure took care'a him.

DAVID *(embarrassed)*: I guess so. I . . . don't want to sound all strange or anything, but I really think God was in front of me, y'know? What I . . . well, what I mean is . . .

JONATHAN: I know what you mean. You're right. Don't forget that. You wouldn't have been able to do that if He wasn't with you.

DAVID *(quickly)*: Exactly. That's what I think too.

JONATHAN: Not that you don't have any talent on your own too.

DAVID: Well, I've been practicing. Out in the field alone and stuff.

JONATHAN: It shows. *(Pause)* My name's Jonathan.

DAVID *(stunned)*: Jonathan? You . . . I mean, your dad's—

JONATHAN: The coach. Yeah, my dad's the coach. *(He laughs.)* But that's my problem, isn't it?

DAVID: He only sent me in 'cuz you couldn't play.

JONATHAN: No, he didn't. He sent you in because he must've thought you could do it. (DAVID *looks very, very uncomfortable.*) Hey, you don't think I'm upset about you out there, do you? (DAVID *is silent.*) You think I'm hacked because I couldn't make the big save? Look, all I care about is we won, y'know.

DAVID: That should'a been yours, though. I feel kind'a bad about that. You're not mad?

JONATHAN: You mean jealous, don't you?

DAVID: Of me? That's a riot!

JONATHAN: No, jealous of what you got to do. *(Pause)*

DAVID: You're not, are you?

JONATHAN: You told me you thought God went ahead of you. You still believe that?

DAVID: I couldn't have done that without Him. I mean, look at me! *(Pulls on his baggy clothes)* You saw that guy!

JONATHAN: So, are you telling me He blessed you out there?

DAVID: Totally.

JONATHAN: So, if He blessed you, you think there's less blessing for me? You think you're that special? (DAVID *is silent.*) God's blessings are limitless, as far as I can tell. He's not likely to run out. So I can enjoy your successes and wait for mine. Then you can celebrate with me. That all right with you?

(DAVID *is quiet for a long moment.*)

DAVID: Are you sayin' you and I could be friends? Come on! I'm the new kid. I don't know the right people. I don't have the right clothes. People already think I look like a geek or something.

JONATHAN: I don't pick my friends by the way they look. *(Puts his hand out)* What's your name anyway?

DAVID: David. David Jesse.

JONATHAN: Well, David, you better get changed. My dad's probably gonna want to talk to you too. I gotta tell ya, he's a little schizo. Watch out for him. (DAVID *laughs.* JONATHAN *takes off his letter jacket and hands it to* DAVID.) Here, put this on. (DAVID *does so, delighted but hesitant.*) That way, nobody'll mess with you. You're probably gonna take some heat for being so good. (DAVID *laughs.*) Yeah. I think you and I are gonna be friends, David. I'll see ya around.

DAVID: See ya, Jonathan.

(JONATHAN *goes out.* DAVID *watches him go, then pulls out a slingshot from under his sweats. He whirls it around and pretends to sail a rock. He leaps in victory and smiles. He tucks the sling away and goes off. The lights fade to:)*

(Blackout.)

Yuke and the Killer Window

A Sketch on Perfectionism
Acts 20:7-12

Running Time

9 minutes

Scene

A youth group meeting room. Evening.

Cast

EUTYCHUS: Also known as "Yuke"; a high-school-age guy or girl
TALETELLER: high school guy or girl

Costume

Modern. Eutychus in Sunday best (if played by a girl, nice slacks).

Props

Folding chairs
Chalkboard
Bible
Date book
Pen
Large storybook
Slide whistle
Windowsill and frame

Production Notes

It can be a lonely life when you think you're indispensable. When you believe that God has called you—and only you—to carry the full weight of His ministry upon your shoulders.

In this modern retelling of Eutychus, we find out it can also be dangerous.

"Yuke and the Killer Window" is modeled after the old "Fractured Fairy Tale" cartoons. There should be a smooth flow between Eutychus and the Taleteller, who trade off the narrative. The windowsill should be high enough for Eutychus to sit on and disappear behind when he drops out of the picture.

(A youth group room. Folding chairs, a chalkboard that says "PIZZA, VOLLEYBALL, AND VIDEO NIGHT—SATURDAY," and a window. At lights, EUTYCHUS is sitting, Bible, open date book, and pen on his lap. He is dead asleep, head back and snoring. The TALETELLER comes in, carrying a large storybook.)

TALETELLER: Once upon a time there was this totally rogue youth group, very much like the one at _____, except that in *this* youth group, all the work was done by one very tired person. And that's just the way he wanted it.

(The stuff on EUTYCHUS's lap slides to the floor. He wakes up, looking around to see if anyone noticed him.)

EUTYCHUS *(rubs his face)*: Hoo boy.

TALETELLER: . . . the young man said, trying desperately to stay awake at a Wednesday evening youth group meeting.

EUTYCHUS: OK. OK, focus. Focus. I can't fall asleep during the special speaker. How wimpy . . . how carnal can you get? *(He zeros in on a "speaker" ahead of him, listening and nodding.)* Yeah. Uh-huh. Oh. I see. Hmmmmm. *(His head slowly nods forward in sleep.)*

TALETELLER *(sitting next to EUTYCHUS)*: Now, this young man's name was pretty bizarre. You see, his parents were on vacation in Greece when the little guy was born and they got a little carried away with the local color and all and they named him Eutychus. Poor kid. Nobody could pronounce it. His friends just called him "Yuke." Short for Ukulele. Some geek in third grade came up with that one.

EUTYCHUS *(head snapping up, eyes wide)*: AMEN! *(Looks around, sheepishly. Smiles at the TALETELLER.)* I . . . ah . . . I thought he had a good point there . . . ah . . . stay awake! Stay awake! *(He leans forward and holds his eyes open with his fingers.)*

TALETELLER: Now, for the last two years, Yuke had been president of the youth group. And everybody agreed, this youth group did more cool stuff than any other in town.

EUTYCHUS: Thirty-two activities this year alone. I made sure of it!

TALETELLER: But everyone also agreed that the group was about as spiritual as a Tupperware party.

EUTYCHUS: Hey, I can't do everything!

TALETELLER: No, but you're gonna give it your best shot.

EUTYCHUS: Oh, great. I've got "Pizza, Volleyball, and Video Night" this weekend. *(Opens his date book)* I still haven't got a total head count, an ad in the paper . . . equipment from the sports closet . . . *(starts to nod off)* . . . paper plates, a video player, a video everyone'll like . . . rides for people who don't have . . . *(He's out and snoring like a bus.)*

TALETELLER: Now, one particular Wednesday evening—right after the joint junior high/high school double overnighter Ping-Pong and ice cream social in the church gym—Yuke had arranged for Pastor Paul, a special speaker from out of town, to come in and speak to the youth group. Yuke needed a break big time, and he knew Paul's sermon "15 Sure-Fire Ways to Godly Living, 30 Ways to Church Harmony, and 101 Ways to Be All Things to All Men" would take up most of the evening. Probably all of the evening.

EUTYCHUS *(wakes up):* Come on! It wouldn't look good for the president of the youth group to look burned out just because he's done 7 car washes, 10 pancake breakfasts, 3 backpack Bible campouts, and planned 4 youth church services all by himself and hasn't slept in two weeks. He needs to . . . *(He goes out in midsentence, head whipping back and mouth wide open. He wakes up with a start.)* OK. OK. OK. I can do this. This is doable. *(Starts pinching his face)* Ah. Oh. Ow. *(He stops. Starts to nod off. Wakes up. Begins pulling on his ears, yanking his hair, bending his fingers back, pulling his eyes open. Looks around.)* Great. I keep doing this, everyone's gonna think I'm possessed. It's hot in here. That's the problem. I'm just a little warm. I'm gonna go sit by the window.

TALETELLER: And so began the beginning of the fall of Yuke the youth group president.

(EUTYCHUS sits by the window and fans himself.)

EUTYCHUS: That's a little better. *(Looks ahead, starts to fade)* Oh, boy. *(Scoots closer to the window)* All right. Preach it, Paul. Yeah. *(Starts to nod off)* This is ridiculous. I gotta have more discipline than this. What kind of youth group leader am I? Gotta be an example. *(He stands near the window.)*

TALETELLER *(halfhearted):* A big mistake. Yuke, don't do it.

EUTYCHUS: Fresh air. Come on. Do it. Do it. *(Starts to slide down the wall. He wakes up.)* OK, OK. More air. Man, is he gonna go on all night? He's said "And finally" about 30 times. *(He climbs up on the windowsill. His Bible slips out of his hand. A slide whistle marks its descent down to the parking lot. Calling out)* Sorry, Mrs. Fambrini!

TALETELLER: Little did he know, Yuke was about to make a real impact on his church body. Believe it or not.

EUTYCHUS *(leans way back):* I promise, I am not doing this again. This is my last year running my tail off so this youth group doesn't look bad. Nobody else wants to do anything. And when they do, I gotta go back behind 'em and make sure it's done right. It seems like I'm the only one who can do things right around here. I guess that's my curse. But it's gonna catch up with me ... someday. *(Starting to fall asleep)* It's gonna . . . kill me, I . . . I can't always drop . . . everything and rescue the program. Your lack of planning is not my emergency. Why's Pastor Paul have to talk so long . . . ? *(Tips dangerously)* Can't help it. Think I'm gonna fall . . . fast a . . . *(Tips out the window)* . . . AHHHHHHHHHHHHHHHHHHHH!

(The slide whistle marks his descent. TALETELLER *goes to the window and looks down. She shakes her head.)*

TALETELLER: Well, Yuke fell dead asleep. Terrible. Three stories down. He just missed Deacon Nerdmann who was carrying a huge pot of decaf coffee and balancing two boxes of Sweet 'n Low on top. It was a painful sight. Little mushy pink packets everywhere. *(She sits on the windowsill.)* Now Pastor Paul and the rest of the youth group heard that Yuke had dropped out, so they rushed downstairs to see if they could bring him back. Paul threw his arms around him, and Yuke was raised to life in front of all of them. The youth group cheered. Nerdmann made another pot of coffee. And besides a headache this big, an occasional bout with insomnia, and a few bruises, Eutychus came through it all without a hitch. Except for one small thing. Eutychus changed his name and from that day on he was no longer known as "Yuke the youth group president" but as "Yuke the delegator."

*(*TALETELLER *closes her book.)*

And the moral of the story is this: Those who carry the world on their shoulders, will feel the pane in the end.

(She smiles as the lights fade to:)

(Blackout.)

Idol Threats

A Sketch on Putting God First
Daniel 3

Running Time

9 minutes

Scene

A TV studio. And a rock concert (on video).

Cast

(Live)
JERALDO: a slimy, stuck-up talk-show host
SHADRACH: a high-school-age guy
MESHACH: a high-school-age girl
ABEDNEGO: a high-school-age guy
DIRECTOR: director of the show

(Video)
ANNOUNCER: high-school-age guy or girl
WORSHIPER: high-school-age guy or girl
CONCERT GOERS: high-school-age teens
SHADRACH
MESHACH
ABEDNEGO

Costume

Modern. The three teens in jeans and casual clothes. Jeraldo in a slick Armani-type suit.

Props

TV
VCR
Remote
3 chairs
Headphones
Cue cards

Production Notes

One has only to look at the front page of the *National Enquirer* while you're checking out your groceries to know that the worship of idols is still in full swing. Our culture seems to demand our bent knees to rock, film, sports, and political celebrities. And we often obey by finding them more interesting and exciting than our own lives in Christ.

Shadrach, Meshach, and Abednego found themselves in a similiar situation in Babylon B.C. With a little updating, we have tried to make their story unfold with modern TV elements.

The studio set doesn't have to have cameras and so forth, just bright spots to give the feel. The VCR portion can be controlled by remote offstage. The rock scene can be created simply with lights and sound and people moving, all looking toward a stage that is never shown. The director can keep the audience clapping with "applause" sign and whirling his finger. Shad, Mesh, and Abe should be normal teens, in stark contrast with what's going on around them.

(In the darkness we see a TV ANNOUNCER *appear on TV monitor and VCR.)*

ANNOUNCER: "Teens who won't bow down to idols." On the next Jeraldo.

(Theme music begins to play. Lights come up, bright. A TV studio. SHAD, MESH, *and* ABE *are sitting in three chairs, center. They are talking with each other, though they can't be heard. The TV monitor and VCR sit downstage. The* DIRECTOR, *in headphones, comes out and signals for the crowd to begin applauding.)*

ANNOUNCER *(on screen)*: He's hip. He's hot. He's hype. He's so awesome, he only has one name. It's Jeraldo. *(Disappears from the screen)*

*(*JERALDO *comes down the center aisle, to applause, with mike in hand. He accepts the applause in obvious self-love, receiving the worship of his audience.* DIRECTOR *keeps the applause coming. Finally* JERALDO *has to make them stop.)*

JERALDO *(as if to a camera)*: Idol worship. Passe? History? A memory of some ancient culture? Or do we see it today. Right here in modern times. In our schools, our churches, our homes. Three teens. Here. In the studio. Who say

"Yes, it's true." Idols. Here to stay. Meet Shadrach. Meshach. Abednego. *(Turning to them)* Welcome.

(Audience applause. JERALDO *moves up onto the stage.)*

SHAD/MESH/ABE *(nodding, smiling):* Hello. Nice to be here, Jeraldo. Thanks for having us, etc.

JERALDO: Idols? Come on. Get real. 20th century. Explain yourselves.

MESHACH: Well, Jeraldo, we don't see idols as just giant golden pigs or anything, y'know. Statues of fat guys doing yoga and stuff, but, like, any time someone replaces God as the center of their attention. Y'know, tries to fill up their lives with something that isn't worthy of it.

SHADRACH: The problem we see, Jeraldo, is it seems our whole society gears us toward worshiping certain people. As if they deserve it because of some special talent the rest of us don't have.

ABEDNEGO: We're told by the media that we should want to be like them. We fantasize about being them.

JERALDO: You mean celebrities. Rock stars. Actors. Writers. Athletes. Zookeepers. Politicians.

ABEDNEGO: Ah . . . exactly.

JERALDO: TV evangelists?

MESHACH: Sometimes. Yes.

ABEDNEGO: What we see is a whole culture of people who can only find their self-worth in someone else. Y'know, in identifying with the way someone else looks, talks, acts. Our own personalities get taken over. What God made us to be gets locked in this desire to be someone else.

MESHACH: Oftentimes because we don't like who we are. We'd rather be someone else.

SHADRACH: And the problem is, when the idolized person fails, it's unacceptable.

MESHACH: It shakes us up because it reminds us of our own weaknesses. So, if we can't find something solid in one celebrity, we go to the next person, until that one falls. Then our life is without meaning again.

JERALDO: Idols. Falling from grace. Scandalous. Inside story. Inquiring minds want to know.

(The three look at each other, quizzically.)

SHADRACH: Well . . . the three of us made a decision to just enjoy the talents of others, the . . . popularity of someone else if they're good at what they do, y'know—

MESHACH: But not to, like, fall down and worship them. Live, eat, and breath them.

ABEDNEGO: Exactly.

JERALDO: Brave kids. Facing the odds. Direct conflict with the world of celebrities. Finally came to a standoff. A showdown. A moment of truth. Talk.

ABEDNEGO: Ah . . . OK. The three of us had gotten tickets to see a band called Nebuchadnezzar. You know the group?

JERALDO: Incredible musicians. Personal friends. Top 40 idols. MTV kings. Princes of the rock world.

ABEDNEGO: OK, you know them. Anyways, we were at the concert, and we looked around and everybody was trying to dress like the lead singer, Blaze Furnace. They were trying to walk like him, talk like him, act like him.

MESHACH: It was sad. Really.

SHADRACH: In the middle of the concert, the band was jammin' pretty good on a song called "Babylon," and Blaze asked us to . . . well, to worship him. It was really scary.

JERALDO: A frightening moment. A test of resolve. We have it on video. Watch the monitor.

(The lights go down. TV screen snaps to life. On video, a group of teen concert-goers are bowing, hands raised, one faints into the arms of another. All this to reggae music. SHADRACH, MESHACH, *and* ABEDNEGO *are looking around, amazed. One* WORSHIPER *grabs* SHADRACH's *arm.)*

WORSHIPER *(on video)*: Bow down, dorks. He's asked us. You're idiots. Blaze is so incredible. What's your problem, anyway?! Don't you just love him! I been livin' for this concert!

(Still on video, SHADRACH, MESHACH, *and* ADEDNEGO *shake their heads and walk out. The camera holds on the bowing audience. The TV screen goes dark. The studio lights come up.)*

JERALDO: Intense. Frightening. Compelling. You lived to tell about it. What happened next?

MESHACH: Well, we weren't very popular.

SHADRACH: Everybody heard about it.

ABEDNEGO: We were right in the middle of it. Things got pretty hot, that's all I can say. But we weren't too worried about it. I mean, we knew who we really worshiped.

JERALDO: Our studio audience is breathless. Our TV audience is frozen in their chairs. I can hardly wait. Spill the beans. Dish the cheese. Who is it?

(The three look at each other again, wondering if JERALDO *has anything between his ears but cue cards.)*

SHAD/MESH/ABE: Jesus Christ.

JERALDO: Oh. *(Pause)* Yes, a . . . a man of integrity. A phenomenal champion of . . . goodwill. And . . . one of my . . . personal heroes. Well, our time is up. Join me tomorrow. Our topic: "Is Elvis Really Working at a Woolworth's Lunch Counter in Biloxi, Mississippi?" Love ya!

(Theme music begins. The DIRECTOR *comes out again and gets the audience to applaud.* SHADRACH, MESHACH, *and* ADEDNEGO *sit there, smiling. The* DIRECTOR *glares at them, trying to get them to applaud.* JERALDO *turns around. His mouth drops open, in shock and offense. Both the* DIRECTOR *and* JERALDO *try to get the young people to stand and applaud as the lights go to)*

(Blackout.)

No Leftovers

A Monologue on Restoration
Acts 12:1-17

Running Time

9 minutes

Scene

A church kitchen. Night.

Costume

Modern

Cast

RHODA: a junior-high or high-school-age girl

Props

Apron
Table
Dirty dishes
Crumbcake

Production Notes

It must have been a little embarrassing for Rhoda to tell a roomful of people that the recently jailed Peter was standing outside, and have them think she was out of her mind. Hurt feelings were bound to show up, as they always do when one is unjustly accused.

In our imagined monologue after the event, we have asked Rhoda to model how conflicts like this should be resolved. Not to hang on to them and let them fester but to honestly confess the feelings. You have no control, really, over the person who wronged you. You can't make him say he's sorry. But you have fulfilled your end of the bargain with God to not let the sun go down on your anger.

Take your time. In playing anger the tendency is to speed through things. Rhoda makes several exits and entrances, so don't be afraid to let the audience think the scene is over, then charge right back in and take stage again.

(A kitchen. There is a table covered with dirty dishes and glasses. RHODA *comes in carrying another armful of dishes. She's wearing a stained apron, her hair messy, and her sleeves rolled up. She sets the dishes down and sees the audience.)*

RHODA: I'm so hopping mad right now I could heave these plates instead of washing 'em. I'm furious! My stomach's in a major knot. I don't even know where to start. *(Looks at the audience)* Just tell me if I don't have a good reason to just walk right in there . . . and . . . and . . . *(She stifles a scream and grabs her hair in clumps.)* DO I LOOK CRAZY TO YOU?! *(Beat)* OK. Forget I asked that. Just remember I'm not. You know that. They should know that by now too. I've been faithfully serving the church leadership at their Prayer and Praise Dinner the first Monday of every month since Easter and getting what for it? Accusations! Humiliation! Jokes on my character! No respect! Honestly, you've gotta be 95 before anyone'll believe a word you have to say. My mother's a great example. Every time I try and tell her how miserable I am at school because I have no friends, she comes up with, "Of course you have friends, honey. Lots of friends. Don't be silly." What am I? Blind? Are these supposedly good friends invisible to only me or what? No way. I'm telling the truth, and just because I'm too young to vote doesn't mean I can't see what's what and be totally honest about it, right? *(Holds up her hand in oath)* Truth: I have no friends at school. And truth: Peter *was* at the door tonight.

(She wipes her hands and goes out. After a few moments, she comes back in with another load of dishes.)

OK, maybe they all were pretty strung out tonight. Y'know, about Peter being thrown in jail and all. I mean, I was upset about it too. When the whole meeting was praying and talking about what we could do to get him out, I was too. Peter's the best preacher we've ever had here. He's taught me more about who Jesus is and how I can, y'know, best serve Him with the way I live my life. My dad was real sure they'd put him away for good to stop him from talking about Jesus. Somehow, deep down, I just knew it wasn't true. We still needed Peter here, and I just didn't think God was gonna take him away. Well, shock-city, right in the middle of serving up the blueberry crumbcake, there's this way soft knock at the back door. Nobody even heard it because they're all yellin' about getting a mass protest together down at the courthouse. So, I go over to the peephole and look out . . . and there's Peter standin' there as plain as day! I could've keeled over on the spot. He looked like he was about to say something, but I didn't *even* give 'im the chance. I ran back into the meeting right in the middle'a one've Elder Blabinga's 20-minute prayers and yelled out, "Hey, guess who's standing at the back door?" Dead silence. Way hostile stares. My dad's all giving me one of those looks that has "on restriction until you die" written all over it. "Peter!" I shouted. "Peter's standing outside right now!" Well, what do you expect? Blabinga throws this major-league fit about having respect for my elders, then my own dad loses it and grabs my arm, "What's your problem, young lady! Coming in here with some childish practical joke! You should be ashamed of yourself!" Then they all said I was crazy. I must'a been seeing angels or something! *(Smiles bitterly)* Y'know, I should'a just brought Peter in in the first place. Right in the middle'a the prayer. No warning. *(Laughs)* It would've been heart attack city with all the pacemakers in there! *(She stops.)* No. I just went back out and brought Peter in; they mobbed him and left me in the dust. No apologies. No, "Hey, Rhoda, we're sorry we thought you were a juvenile delinquent without a responsible bone in your body." So now, I'm still in here, washing *their* dirty dishes and so hacked I can't even think straight. I'm still shaking.

(Suddenly, she stops and storms out of the kitchen, only to storm back in a second later.)

OK, this is what gets me. They hurt my feelings big time. And they embarrassed me to no end. Especially when my dad just jumped right in. Of all people, he should know I wouldn't make something up. He should've known me better and just . . . believed me.

(Stifles back tears. Suddenly she picks up a plate and is about to heave it. She stops. She sets it down.)

I heard my dad say something one time. He said that people shouldn't let the sun go down on their anger. Deal with it. Man, I should just go back in there and tell them they hurt my feelings. How I feel. Sure, Peter's a major deal, but my feelings are a big deal too. *(She stands and turns to go.)* No. They'll think I'm ridiculous. I mean, what if they don't see they hurt my feelings and apologize? I'll just be standing there, looking like an idiot. *(She comes back to the table and starts to arrange plates. She stops.)* No. It doesn't matter what they say. I can't make them feel bad about it. What matters is they know how I feel. That's all I have to do. The rest is up to them. OK. All right. I'll be right back.

(She sets the plates down and marches off. After a few moments, she walks back in. She looks shocked. She goes to the table in silence. She starts stacking dishes. She stops.)

My dad apologized. Totally. In front've everyone. This is a cause to party. *(She picks up a blueberry crumbcake and starts to eat it. Then she laughs.)* By the way, I'm off restriction.

(As she eats, the lights fade to:)

(Blackout.)

In Deep

A Monologue on Recognition
Genesis 37

Running Time

7 minutes

Scene

A hole somewhere. Evening.

Cast

JOSEPH: a high-school-age guy

Costume

Modern

Production Notes

Though based on the Old Testament story of how Joseph was thrown down into the cistern by his jealous brothers, "In Deep" is really about anyone who has found himself in too far and recognizes that God is his only hope for salvation and restoration.

In production, the cistern can be created by either a circle of light that Joseph can't transgress, or a circle of rope or tape to signify the dimensions.

Attention should be paid to the mime work as Joseph visually establishes for us the hole he has gotten himself into. Note the desperation and the continual looking up for salvation.

(JOSEPH *standing alone onstage. He is hemmed in by a circle of light.*)

JOSEPH: What a hole this is. (*He looks around. He examines the height of the walls, the size of the space, the dirt on the floor.*) I've really gotten myself in deep this time. Major league. Oh, man . . . (*He looks up, peering.*) I can't even see a way out. Somewhere up there. (*He mimes trying to climb one of the walls.*) I . . . how did I . . . I was just . . . (*He falls back to the floor.*) What a pit! I don't deserve this. (*Shouting up*) I DON'T DESERVE THIS! It isn't fair. I'm harmless. Even if I was wrong, I didn't mean it. I was just messing around. I didn't mean to hurt anyone. (*Up*) I DIDN'T MEAN TO HURT ANYONE. (*Sighs*) Least of all myself. But now . . . (*Pause*) I'm sunk. I think this is it. I am totally sunk. (*Pause*) I've got to figure something out. I gotta think. (*Stands and paces*) OK, how'd this happen to me? I was cool, wasn't I? Totally in control. My life was just fine. (*Stops*) I guess I let it go on too long. Let it go too far. Why didn't I see this coming?! What a total idiot I am. Idiot. I'm so stupid, stupid . . . jerk. (*Goes to the wall*) Get out. I've gotta get out. (*He maniacally examines the walls, trying to find a place for a foothold.*) Come on . . . come on! I can't stay down here! I can't. No way . . . no way . . . There's no way! (*Slapping the wall and the ground*) Great! Just great! I've dug my own grave! (*Stops*) I need help. Help . . . HELP! HELP! (*Realizes something*) There's no one out there I trust. No one up there. They're all into their own stuff. Their own worlds. There's only one person who could . . . help me. But he's . . . I think he's . . . (*Decides to try. Calls out.*) FATHER . . . ? (*Whispers*) Father, can you hear me?! (*Loud*) I need you! I need help! I'm so alone in here. I can't do it . . . I can't get out by myself. YOU'RE GONNA HAVE TO COME DOWN HERE AND GET ME! I . . . hope you're listening, 'cuz I am in deep this time, Father. (*Listens for a moment. No reply. No earth-shattering notice. He sighs and makes a smooth place on the ground. He kneels, wrapping his arms around himself.*) Getting dark. Getting cold. (*Calming himself*) I'll be OK. OK, OK, OK. All right. I'll be fine. I don't like this. At all. But I'll live. I feel like I'm the only person in the world, but I'll live. I think . . . somehow I feel like you heard me. I'm not as . . . shaky. I'm . . . I'll just wait for you. I'll live through this night. I'll . . . survive. You're working on it, aren't you. I know you are, 'cuz you're my only hope. You're my only . . . (*Looks up*) FATHER!

(*The lights fade to*)

(*Blackout.*)

Dead to the World

A Monologue on New Life
Mark 5:21-43

Running Time

11 minutes

Scene

A youth group retreat. Day.

Cast

JAIRUS' DAUGHTER: a high-school-age girl

Costume

Modern

Props

A chair
Bottled water

Production Notes

The raising of Jairus' young daughter in the Gospels is such an apt image of being made alive in Christ. This monologue explores the metaphor by dealing with what we do in our lives that is death-producing, and what we take on that is life-giving. We are all created with a built-in longing for God. When God is not found, we fill that urging void with what we can find around us—food, drugs, sex, relationships, etc.

Here, JAIRUS' DAUGHTER speaks candidly with her peers, identifying with them, challenging them not to fill up their lives with things that make them feel dead. But instead to take Jesus up on His call to "Be alive!" We have tried to give a realistic view of her conversion couched in modern language and issues.

This monologue should play with all the sincerity of a spontaneous testimony. Very natural and not overearnest and preachy. Take your time.

(At lights, JAIRUS' DAUGHTER [J. D.] is sitting on a chair in the playing area. She's drinking bottled water.)

J. D. (leans forward and smiles): What do you think of your life? Right now. This minute. Go ahead. Think about it.

(She pauses for a good 30 seconds.)

Like it? Things going pretty well for you? Or is your phenomenal life punctuated with little irritations like—you hate yourself, you hate your parents, everybody you know seems to hate you. Or, maybe people really like you, you have a great relationship with the folks, and you can get the grades pretty easily. But you just can't seem to keep a boyfriend or a girlfriend for more than three days.

(Pause. She leans back, pointing out into the audience.)

You. You think everybody else thinks you're huge and you should spend your college savings on liposuction. And you. You'd do whatever it takes to maintain that rogue reputation with those dudes around you. You. You're wondering if you're ever going to feel really happy. And you—you'd do just about anything to get some really hip clothes. Even rip 'em off. And a lot of you—I'd say a lot of you sitting in this room right now—have this huge empty space inside that's just eating you alive. You don't feel it in there? You don't think I know what I'm talking about? I'll tell you what I think. I think the only reason you *don't* feel it is because you keep yourself so filled up with friends, and school, and TV, and parties, and telephone calls, and backseats of cars, and food, and dope, and beer. Anything you can get your hands on just so you don't have to *feel* anything. No? Well. Trust me. I know about you, and I know about me.

(Small pause. She takes a drink of bottled water.)

There are some people in this room who've felt the way I've felt. Some of you are feeling it right now. So bad you just wanna die. Or maybe you already just feel dead. You look OK on the outside, right? But you haven't felt really happy or really sad or really anything for such a long time you're just going through the motions. Something inside has died, and it's really stinking up the place. Well, I can smell it. I can smell dead . . . because I've been there. Dead, I mean. It wasn't so long ago that I don't remember what it was like.

(She sighs. Takes another drink.)

Before I . . . died, I was way into it like some of you. I could go into details and tell you exactly what I was filling myself up with, but you get the idea. I was just like some of you with the joint in your pocket, the bottle in your glovebox, the pornography under your bed, the laxatives in your purse, the "precaution" in your wallet. And I knew what you know about what all of that does to you . . . eventually. Yeah, and I even knew somebody you think you might know. I knew Jesus. No, really. I knew Him. My dad used to go and listen to Him teach. Dad was way into Him. He'd come home and talk nonstop at dinner about Him—what Jesus said, what Jesus did, who Jesus was. I don't know if your parents talk nonstop about God or what, but I was getting real deaded out on the whole routine.

(She laughs softly to herself. Takes another drink.)

One day I woke up with the flu. Y'know how you can kind'a feel it comin' on. Well, I woke up wasted. Really sick. I couldn't even sit up or anything. I guess my resistance was down from all the stuff I was doin' or something, but it got so bad I don't remember anything past that morning—anything real, I mean. The last thing I knew, my dad was going to find Jesus to bring Him to our house and ask Him to heal me. I'd never seen my dad look so scared. I remember knowing in this totally complete way that I wouldn't see my parents again. Or my friends. That I'd never get a second chance to . . . tell them I loved them, make them proud of me . . . or to just . . . really live for a change. I passed out asleep. I was dead to the world. I can't remember anything. Except someone telling me to get up. It was far away. It was a voice I didn't know. "She's not dead, she's asleep," He was saying. Of course I was just asleep, wasn't I? I mean, what else? "Little girl, get up," the voice said. I knew my dad must've found Jesus. It was His voice. Once you hear it, you never forget it, that's for sure. The room crashed in on me. I sat up. Jesus was there. I knew He knew all about me. No use hiding. What I had done wouldn't embarrass or frighten Him. And with all that, He wanted to give me another life. One that was worth living. One that . . . well, for starters, was valuable enough that He took time out to spark it back to life. Turn it in a new direction. I knew I'd gotten another chance.

(She sighs again. Takes a drink. She smiles.)

I know I'm a rare case. But being dead once has really made me want to live. I mean really live. Not exist. Not numb out. Not fill every pain or emptiness I have with something that keeps me dead. Oh, believe me, the temptation is still there to do things that make me feel dead. And, think about it, a lot of the stuff you do that makes you feel alive really ends up deading you out, right? Well, I'll tell you the secret. That empty spot is for Jesus. He'll fill it up. You don't have to find stuff for it. And when I feel like, quick, I need some- thing to fill it, I can talk to Jesus about it before it kills me. Again. *(Chuckles)* Y'know, I've got more life than I can deal with now, between my own and His in me. He brought me back, y'see. He loves me a lot more than I love myself. But that's coming around too. Well . . . I guess that's all. Thanks for listening.

(She nods, smiles, and takes a drink of bottled water as the lights fade to:)

(Blackout.)

YOU CAN GET THERE FROM HERE

Five Sketches and Monologues on Surviving the Teen Years

"You Can Get There from Here" brings together more of the evangelistic sketches and monologues of this collection. Most of the scenes have been designed with a very realistic approach in mind and with a desire to create an accurate picture of what it's like to struggle with life in a very difficult period of change—and in a world that doesn't make things any easier.

"You Can Get There from Here" is a mixture of plays designed for churched groups, audiences of varying faith backgrounds, and for evangelism. You'll find topics like sexual boundaries ("One More"), suicide ("Fade to Black"), self-esteem ("Barre Exam"), and the ministry of others in the Christian's life ("You Can Get There from Here"). There's also a monologue series called "Scars," which takes in many of the above ideas and folds them in with issues like divorce, drugs, anxiety, loneliness, and shame.

Like "Yuke and the Killer Window" and "Warmwater, Illinois," these sketches and monologues can be performed separately or in an evening of all five. To that end, we've arranged them in the order we think will work best. If you decide to do them all, you'll have a program that lasts about an hour. Also, because some set changes will be required, you might consider planning to use music in between scenes.

The separate pieces last from 9 to 18 minutes and cover the range of styles.

All the parts can be played by junior high, senior high, and college-age actors. If older actors are available, there are several roles throughout the five scenes in which they can be cast.

Also, if you don't desire or don't have the resources to stage these plays, they will work well if they are just read aloud—particularly the monologues in "Scars," "Barre Exam," "One More," and "Fade to Black." Discussion can then follow.

We pray God's grace for you as you set out to catch hearts and minds for the gospel.

You Can Get There from Here

A Sketch on Not Getting There All by Yourself

Running Time

14 minutes

Scene

A stage. Anytime.

Cast

GUY: a high-school-age guy or girl
FRIEND: a high-school-age guy or girl
YOUTH LEADER: a young man or woman
DAD: a man in his 40s
MOM: a woman in her 40s
BABY BROTHER: a child
NEEDY PERSON: a man or woman of any age
GRANDMOTHER: a woman in her 70s
GOD: a man or woman of any age
BODY OF CHRIST (1) ⎫
BODY OF CHRIST (2) ⎬ a man or woman of any age
BODY OF CHRIST (3) ⎭

Note: Since the characters are all representations, they can be played by all high-school-age actors in makeup and costume or by actors closer to the characters' ages.

Costume

Modern

Props

12 black rehearsal blocks
4 planks
1 ladder
Signs identifying characters
Big black Bible
Cane

Production Notes

It seems to be the American myth that we need to stand alone. The John Waynes have provided us with the image that we don't need help from anyone. We are self-sufficient individuals cut adrift in a universe where everything depends on us.

The Bible gives us a different portrait of life. We are provided with the image of a body with many members. This is essentially a message of hope for Christians. We don't have all the answers, all strength, all perseverance. But Christ does, and oftentimes He offers this to us through those around us.

This is the message of "You Can Get There from Here," in which a teenager finds assistance and navigation from a variety of sources. It is saying there is no shame in reliance. It doesn't have to depend all on you. God provides many people in our lives who purposely or unknowingly provide just the missing piece of the life puzzle.

Cues must be tight in this play. Those entering in on GUY's travels need to be there at the appointed moment. The setting of the blocks can vary depending on the size of the playing area. If there is room, you can really spread them out. If there isn't, set them out mazelike, making use of the depth, so GUY is traveling up and down stage and not so much across it.

(Rehearsal blocks scattered all around the playing area, a good distance from each other and in different directions. One might be able to jump from block to block—if he was wearing a red and blue costume and spun webs from his wrists.

(At lights, GUY is sitting on the first block, downstage right. He looks dejected, head in hands and staring at the floor. He looks up, sees the sprawl of blocks ahead of him. He looks at the audience and sighs.)

GUY *(sings):* "Do you see what I seeeee." Kind of discouraging, isn't it? Oh, some of you adults don't remember this scene, do you? The first act of a play you'd kind'a like to forget. Well, it's a little hard to forget when you're sitting where I am. *(Stands)* OK, lemme explain this to you. This is what it's like to be a teenager, got it? It's s'posed to be symbolism, OK? *(Raps on the block)* These are places we're s'posed to be. Solid ground, so t'speak. But, you're not really sure how to get to 'em. You could jump, if your name was Kareem,

I guess. You could also forget you had anywhere to go by sleeping, drinking, toking, snorting, etc. But, the blocks are kind'a there permanently, so when you wake up . . . surprise, surprise.

(He sits back down with a sigh.)

A small part of me just wants to sit here, but I kind'a have this vision . . . *(does "Twilight Zone" theme)* . . . of what I wanna be like. Oh, I'm OK, I guess. I just wanna go somewhere while I'm here. Problem is, I just can't figure out how to get going. Where to get going, y'know? *(Drops his head in his hands again. Seems to get lost in depression.)* I'm just not sure I can get there from here. At least not all by myself. *(Sighs again and stares at the floor)*

(A girl wearing the sign FRIEND *enters. She carries a long plank of wood, which she holds between the first block and the next. She smiles at the audience, then lets it drop. The sound wakes* GUY *up. He looks at her, then at the plank. She smiles and nods. He stands on the block and steps out onto the plank, hesitantly.* FRIEND *goes out.* GUY *is a little shaky, but he crosses to the next block.)*

GUY: Wheew! I did it. One giant step for me, one small step for teenagekind. It makes me feel like there's no turning back now. It's weird what a little push from a good friend can do for you. I'm not sure I would've done it without her. *(Pause. He looks around.)* Where am I? Wait a minute . . . this is really unfamiliar terrain. It's a little scary. *(Looks back)* Maybe I should . . . naaah.

*(*GUY *turns around. Someone with the sign* YOUTH LEADER *is standing there holding a plank. He waits.* GUY *nods his head.* YOUTH LEADER *smiles and sets the plank down between two blocks and goes out.)*

GUY: I always liked him *(her)*. Things get a little spooky, and a little confusing, and it's nice to have someone to talk to who isn't so . . . afraid of the dark. Or maybe he's *(she's)* still a little afraid, but he's *(she's)* been in the room a little longer. But this . . . this feels great. Phenomenal. I'm really cooking with gas now! *(He looks back.)* Not bad! Not bad at all!

(When he turns back around, three people are standing there with a sign that reads FAMILY. GUY *halts, with one foot off the block. Like a hand pushed him back.)*

GUY: Why is it so hard to keep moving at home? I know my family is necessary, but you guys can be one major drag!

(One of the FAMILY *crosses his arms like dad, the other points a finger like mom, the third sticks a tongue out like baby brother Herman.)*

Whoa. Brutal. Sometimes I feel like I'm going backward at home, y'know. There's just so much daily stuff. Conflict. Bickering. Details. Beg for the car keys, turn down your CD player, clean your room, give me back my favorite sweatshirt, I don't do lima beans and I never have, don't touch that remote or you're dead meat, toad breath! Whoaaaa. *(Catches his breath.* FAMILY *goes back to normal.)* Ah, they're not so bad. But I think it's time for a little growth here.

(GUY *leaps to the next block but doesn't make it. He crashes to the floor in a heap.*)

GUY: Wasted. The agony of defeat.

(*The* FAMILY *comes forward and helps him to his feet. When he's standing,* DAD *puts his arm around him and gives him a hug,* MOM *starts brushing him off and fixing his clothes,* BABY BROTHER *clucks his tongue and shakes his head like "Are you the major doofus of the universe, or what?"*)

GUY: Thanks. Thanks a lot. I'm fine.

(DAD *steps back.* MOM *keeps brushing* GUY *off, until he looks at her like "Puh-leeze." She steps back, smiling. He shows* BABY BROTHER *his fist. He scoots back to the* FAMILY. *They go out.*)

GUY: Guess I'm in no-man's-land here. Well, here goes. (*He climbs up onto the next block.*) OK, that was good for me. A couple'a scrapes, a couple'a bruises, but I'm all right. It stretched my character. Built some strength. It tested my faith. That's what it did. OK. I need more of that. I need my faith to be tested some more.

(*In comes someone wearing the sign* NEEDY PERSON *and carrying a plank.*)

GUY: Great. Be careful what you ask for. OK, OK, this is doable. It's the next step. I can see that. Definitely. And it is a doozy. But I've always been such a sponge. I've always been the one that needed stuff. Then there's this guy. What do I do? (*Clears his throat*) Can . . . can I help you?

(NEEDY PERSON *smiles and sets the plank down.* GUY *crosses, tentatively, and shakes his hand.* NEEDY PERSON *goes out.* GUY *takes in a deep breath.*)

GUY: That felt good. I feel good. The more I gave, the more I felt satisfied. Bizarre. Did I just say satisfied? Isn't that what I wanted all along? Does that mean I've arrived?

(*He turns around and sees two blocks, equidistant but in two different directions.*)

GUY: Wonderful. Now I gotta make a choice. (*Turns one way, then another*) Both look good to me. Or they're both bad. How am I supposed to know? I'M JUST A KID! OK, OK. What I need is some . . . whadd'ya call it . . . perspective! I got no perspective here. I need to somehow, get above it and get a clearer view

(*Someone wearing the sign* GRANDMOTHER *comes in, bent with age, walking with a cane and carrying a Bible.*)

GUY: Hi, Gram. What're you doin' here? (GRANDMOTHER *walks silently up to* GUY *and hands him her cane and Bible.*) What's up, Gram? You OK? Gram? Gram? (GRANDMOTHER *has gone out.*) Grams is up there, y'know. Sometimes she goes a little off the deep—

(GRANDMOTHER *reenters with an A-frame ladder. GUY's mouth drops open.* GRANDMOTHER *stands the ladder down, pops it open. Then she pats one of the steps, takes the Bible and cane from* GUY, *pats him on the cheek, affectionately, and goes out.*)

GUY *(after her)*: Grams, you're too cool. *(To the audience)* Sometimes help comes from places you didn't expect. Or just plain didn't think about. *(He climbs up on the ladder and looks down on the blocks.)* Well, it still looks like one doozy of a decision, but I think I got just the advice I needed. Yeah, that's the way I'm goin', all right. *(He climbs down, closes the ladder, then lays it between two blocks. He climbs across on all fours and reaches the block.)* This feels great. I really feel like I've made a lot of progress. But I want to keep going. *(Stands)* I feel real strong. Real secure. *(He looks ahead. The next block is way beyond reach.)* How am I supposed to get to that? Come on, that is imposeeeblay. *(He sighs.)* Maybe I could pole-vault it? Maybe . . . maybe Scotty can beam me over there. Where's the Enterprise when you really need it? *(He stops.)* That just gave me an idea. *(He closes his eyes for a moment, then opens them.)* No, I'm not checking out. I thought I'd give this one a little prayer. *(He closes his eyes again, then opens them. He looks around.)* Nope. I'm still here. I thought maybe there'd be a little miracle action, y'know. No such luck, I guess. *(He looks back to the block he came from.)* Maybe if I went back there and, like, got a running start I could jump from—

(Three people come in carrying blocks. Each wears a sign: BODY, OF, CHRIST. GUY *freezes in total surprise. They smile at him, wave, and set the blocks down, making it short hops to where* GUY *is going. They wave again and go out.)*

GUY: Amazing. A total surprise. I never thought they even noticed me. Just another kid in the youth group or somethin'. And now, look at this! *(Calling off)* You like me. You really like me! OK. Let's get a move on. *(He makes the short jumps to each block and lands on the fourth. He does a little victory dance, like he just made the final touchdown of the game. He doesn't see the final block setting ahead of him.)* Incredible! Phenomenal! Radical! This is where I wanted to be. All along. I've arrived. I'm here. I'm just gonna hang right here. I like it right where I am!

(As he speaks, someone with the sign reading GOD *comes in, carrying a plank.* GOD *watches* GUY *for a few moments.)*

GUY *(looking back)*: I never thought I'd get here from there. Look how far back that is. I can hardly see it. I'm a lot stronger than I thought. I'm not bad. Not bad at all. Maybe I should just write a book or somethin' tellin' other people how to get here— *(*GOD *sets the plank between the blocks with a distinct whack, then goes out.* GUY *hears the crack of wood. He looks around. He sees the plank.)* How'd that get there? Hello? Hello?! *(He squats down and touches it. Suddenly he stands.)* This feels right. I need to move on. I'm a little scared, though. *(He steps out onto the wood, he is a little unstable, like a tightrope* *walker losing his balance. Finally, he is up straight. He looks ahead.)* I don't know where this is going. *(He begins firm, well-placed steps. The lights are beginning to fade.)* I do know who put it there. And who'll still be there on the other side. I gotta tell ya. I'm excited about this.

(As GUY *continues to walk, the lights go to:)*

(Blackout.)

Fade to Black

A Sketch on Teen Suicide for Stage and Video

Running Time

9 minutes

Scene

Shryl's bedroom. Evening.

Cast

(Live)
SHYRL: a high-school-age girl

(Video)
SHYRL
MOM: a woman in her 40s
LITTLE SISTER: a junior-high- or high-school-age girl
BEST FRIEND: a high-school-age girl
HUNK: a high-school-age guy
MITCH: a high-school-age guy

Costume

SHYRL in casual hip dress. MOM, LITTLE SISTER, BEST FRIEND, and HUNK in nice, black clothes that might be worn to a funeral. Mitch in casual, very geeky clothes.

Props

Chair
Nightstand

Coatrack
Various items of clothing and jackets
TV
VCR
Walkman with headphones
Magazine

Production Notes

The statistics are staggering. Suicide is the number one cause of death among teenagers. This suggested to us that not everyone who attempts or succeeds in such self-destruction is an unusually broken person. With such a high percentage of deaths, we considered how many may have given up on life without what an adult might consider a heavy traumatic experience.

Maybe they just found out life isn't what they expected. Or they can't seem to find some kind of overriding satisfaction. Or they're depressed over something that may appear transient to parents but stands for something quite significant without the years of adult perspective. Or maybe they simply think no one cares—really cares. And, sadly enough, suicide is a powerful way to make people suffer for not showing their love.

In any of these cases, children and teens are listening to lies. And that's just what Shyrl discovers in "Fade to Black." Lies abound everywhere about what life is supposed to be, and only Jesus Christ offers the complete truth.

A good portion of this sketch is done on video and tight, crisp segues need to be achieved from live to tape. The characters who appear on the TV need to be shot in "talking head" format—only head and shoulders on screen. The video can be controlled by remote offstage. Shyrl plays the part very blithely, it appears, until her "lies" speech, when she reveals how serious her situation really is.

(A chair, covered with clothes. A nightstand. A coatrack hung with jackets. A TV and a VCR are facing the audience. At lights, SHYRL *is sitting on the floor, an arm draped across the chair. She is listening to her Walkman and singing way too loud and way out of tune. She is flipping through a magazine, distractedly. We listen to her for a few moments, then she looks up.)*

SHYRL *(too loud):* My mom named me Cheryl. *(Stops)* Is it too loud? Am I too— *(Pulls the headphones off)* My mom named me Cheryl. No, it couldn't be something cool like Tiffany, Ashleigh, or . . . Nina. Nothing even close. Just Cheryl. Snoozer city. So, last year I just started spelling it S. H. Y. R. L. It works. Try it. No vowels, I know. But it works. Remember "A, E, I, O, U, and sometimes Y." My mom gagged over it. I told her to deal. My dad thinks it looks like some Russian name or something. I told him he could hang with it. It was fun for a week, then it got routine. Like everything else. That's the whole problem. Stuff gets ordinary. Real fast. Like your favorite cassette. You play it every minute you breathe. You cannot, repeat, cannot live without hearing that tape every second. Then one day, you hate it. You think if you ever hear it again, you'll throw up for an hour. *(She pops the headphones back on and listens for a long few moments, then she stops.)* Like this cassette. *(She hits "eject," pulls the tape and sails it across the room.)* Barf city. I feel the same way about Snickers bars, Dove Bars, Pee Wee Herman, Michael Jackson, and Suzuki Samurais. I used t'love 'em all. Now . . . gag-o-rama. *(She pops another tape into the Walkman.)* Lately, I've been starting to feel that way about life. *(On goes the headphones, and she starts bopping to the beat.)*

(The TV suddenly springs on. This is SHYRL's *brain and imagination. We see a talking head video of* SHYRL.)

SHYRL *(on video):* I've been feelin' burned out for a long time. Since the start of sophomore year, prob'ly. I figured I was just ticked off. Ticked off 'cuz this didn't happen, or I couldn't do that. Like most people. Like my mom who is always perpetually hacked. She was gonna be a dancer or somethin', now she's a caterer. Anyway, I didn't think I was all that bad, until one day I was sitting waitin' for the bus to school. It was raining kind'a hard. Mitch the Weenie was sitting next to me blabbering about something. It was like his voice was just thumping in my ear. Like a bass. All I was doing was staring at the bus. The front looked like a face. All wet. It was getting closer. Moving kind'a fast in the rain. Smiling.

SHYRL *(live; dropping the headphones):* And all I could think of was, "Why don't I just step in front of it." It was like a voice. "Last stop, Shyrl, just stand up and walk." Driver wouldn't be able to stop in time. Be all his fault. He's a jerk, anyway, the way he flirts with anything wearing a jean skirt. Then I wouldn't have to worry about being so . . . irritated all the time. Disappointed by stuff I expect. Stuff that doesn't come through like promised. I wouldn't have to get hurt. I'd stop getting depressed and making my parents freak out. It seemed easier. I wasn't scared. I stood up. I walked to the curb. Mitch was sayin' something dorky. My face felt like it couldn't move. *(Stares off, distracted)* And I started thinking . . . I was thinking . . .

(Video comes on.)

SHYRL *(on video):* I was . . . y'know, imagining what people I knew would say about me. When they heard the news. When they found out that poor little Shyrl was . . . gone. Wasted by a school bus. I imagined how they'd be so . . . sad. And how I wouldn't be such a disappointment to people anymore.

SHYRL *(live):* Like . . . like my mom.

MOM *(on video):* By a school bus?! Just great. She had to do it in front of the whole world. She was always trying to embarrass me. Spelled her perfectly fine name like she was from another planet or something. Never liked anything. No pleasing her. Not like her little sister. Now there's a good kid for you.

(LITTLE SISTER's *face appears on the video.*)

LITTLE SISTER *(on video):* Shyrl. You were always so bizarre. And you used to call *me* weird? Well, at least I can *finally* get all mom's attention, like I deserve. By the way, thanks for the Madonna CDs. And the Walkman.

SHYRL *(live):* You keep your hands off my CDs, you little brat!

BEST FRIEND *(on video):* Shyrl was my best friend. I've known her since second grade. She had an attitude sometimes. People liked her more than she thought they did. She also used to think I tried to steal her boyfriends. I never did. They always just liked me more.

SHYRL *(live):* Get outta town! You were always trying to—

HUNK *(on video):* Shyrl did what?

SHYRL *(live):* Mark Baxter! Major hunk.

HUNK *(on video):* That is really a drag. You know, I was trying to get up enough nerve to ask her out. Now I'll never get the chance. I am so bummed.

SHYRL *(live):* No, wait! Mark! I didn't do it! *(Crawling toward the TV)* I'm free on Friday night! All day Saturday and Sunday after church . . .

(Too late. His face has disappeared. SHYRL *sits. Her face pops up on the screen. They stare at each other a long time.)*

SHYRL *(video):* That's when you knew you were lying.

SHYRL *(live; quietly):* Yes.

(SHYRL *disappears from the screen.*)

SHYRL *(live):* That's when I knew I was lying. What I mean to say is: I was believing lies. I was believing lies that said life was supposed to always go my way, when it doesn't. I was believing lies that said if everyone didn't like me, I must be unlikable. That if someone thought I was stupid, then I was stupid. If someone didn't think I was pretty, then I must be ugly. I believed that if I got hurt, I could never survive. That if I was treated badly, I deserved it. That if I could beat someone to the insult, I would be saved from the humiliation. I believed that when my parents were distant, it was my fault. That if they hurt me, they didn't really love me. I believed the lie that if I didn't think God protected me, then He must not really be there. I believed the lie that said if life was hard, it would always be hard. That if it was hard for a long time, it was better to give up. I believed that if I felt pain, nobody else did. I believed if I wanted to end it all, it was my business. And I really believed the lie that nobody cared. Well I know two people who do care if I live: Jesus Christ and me. Even if no one else does, that is enough. And that is the truth.

(Long pause. She stands.)

The last thing I knew, Mitch the Weenie was pulling at my arm, "What're you doing?! What're you doing?!" he kept shouting. He tried to pull me back from the street. "There's a puddle. The bus is going to splash you!" It was too late. Mud and water splashed all over my new Guess jeans. I didn't care. I was laughing. It just came out of me. I turned and looked at Mitch.

(MITCH *appears on the screen—a geek if there ever was one—looking at* SHYRL *like she's insane.*)

I was so happy, I just wanted to plant a big one on him, y'know. *(She looks at the TV, then at the audience.)* Then I came to my senses.

(SHYRL *puts her Walkman on the chair and walks out.* MITCH *disappears from the screen. After a moment,* SHYRL *appears on the TV. She smiles. The lights fade to blackout. We see her face smiling in the darkness, then the TV screen goes dark.*)

One More

A Monologue on Sexual Boundaries

Running Time

9 minutes

Scene

A kitchen. Saturday night.

Cast

JESSICA: a high-school-age girl

Costume

Casual jeans and dark-colored blouse or sweatshirt dusted with flour.

Props

Kitchen table
Baking supplies: flour and sugar cannisters, bowls, spoons, etc.
Plate of four large cookies visibly made with M&Ms
Large portable tape deck/stereo

Production Notes

Sexual boundaries. It's an uncomfortable topic, but one that we can't afford not to discuss. This is one area where what you don't know will hurt you. Sexuality is an area where many lies are told, and many lies believed because it's tied up with our fragile emotions and self-esteem. Teens and adults alike need to hear over and over the honest fact that our sexuality was not created for casual use or as a means of bolstering our sinking and distorted view of ourselves.

Jessica in the following sketch "One More" struggles with the fundamental issue of how we can fool ourselves into intimacy. I thought saying no to intimate sexuality outside of a committed married relationship was the right answer, she says. But in the heat of the moment—and under duress by a boyfriend, the media, and a permissive society—she finds out that, apparently, it's the wrong answer.

A lie if there ever was one. And the truth needs to be told.

"One More" is a poignant monologue about Jessica's sexual experiences. It's very forthright. It doesn't pay not to be anymore. There is no mention of Jesus in the monologue. Jessica doesn't know Him, so His influence can't be felt in the portrait. And although this piece can well be used in an evangelistic setting, don't fool yourself by thinking Christian young people don't need to hear it either. Sexuality is one area where people often don't let Christ come near.

As it's been said in other notes, take your time with this one. A good balanced pace will need to be found in order to time eating the cookies with what's being talked about. The monologue begins very casually, getting more and more intense as we move along. This is by design and needs to be handled with sensitivity.

This sketch is not for entertainment. It must include Bible-based teaching on sexual boundaries and sexuality.

(JESSICA *is sitting at the kitchen table. It's covered with baking stuff—flour, sugar, bowls. She's been making cookies.*

(Flour is clinging to her blouse, with a touch or two on her face. There is a plate of four cookies sitting in front of her.)

JESSICA *(holds up the plate):* I'm saving these for someone special. *(She laughs.)* Peanut butter and oatmeal cookies, with M & Ms, raisins, and white chocolate chips. Radical, huh? Double-stuff Oreos can eat exhaust on this one. These puppies will catch you a sugar buzz like you never had. Can you believe it? I haven't had a single one. I don't look like it, do I? I'm trying to be careful with this stuff. *(Laughs)* I didn't make a whole lot, anyways. Just a couple of batches. My mom's gonna take some to her work on Monday. My two little brothers ate the rest of 'em while I was in the bathroom. 15 cookies between the two of 'em, gone before the little M & Mers knew what hit 'em. *(Taps the plate)* But I saved these. They're mine to give away to someone special, whoever I want. *(She stands, looks herself over.)* Boy, what a mess I am.

(She goes offstage. Comes back a moment later with a boom box. She sets it on the table, turns on a station, and starts to clean up, taking her time.)

Baking. Can't you just believe it? On a Saturday night, no less. That's what happens when you eat too many cookies. Porker city and it's a date with your ever-loving family every night of the week. I deserve it. *(Pushing the lid down on the flour cannister)* Honestly, I could just kill myself sometimes the way I lose control. *(Pushes her hair back)* Y'know, I can remember when Saturday nights didn't mean a thing. They came and went, and you watched TV and stuff and that was that. Now, it's like, some all-important night. Like you judge how great your life is by what happens on your Saturday nights. It started one Saturday when I noticed it was getting dark and I got this pain. This . . . hurting. I cried and cried. "Wait till you get dates," my mom said. "You're just growing up and you want to go on dates. It'll happen." But Mom's forgetting something. You can want dates, but somebody's gotta ask ya out. That's kind'a the way the whole thing works. I just wanted someone to notice me. Forget a date, y'know, just . . . flirt with me. I'd've done just about anything for that. Mom didn't help with her "maybe you're doin' something to scare 'em off" comments. Then I met Teddy. *(Without thinking, she picks up one of the cookies and eats as she talks.)* He asked me to go see some Sylvester Stallone film. I don't even remember what it was. I was so grateful, y'know. He was like . . . lookin' for me after class, waitin' around for me. I could've died. We went out a couple of weeks, and one night we were studying together and he started . . . putting his hands . . . on me. I was excited . . . and afraid . . . and, I don't know. I don't want to say relieved. But someone thought I was attractive, y'know. I felt guilty, but I let him do it. I'm thinking, this is what I have to do. It's what he expects. *(She begins eating another cookie.)* This was makin' out, right? No big. Everyone makes out. I know that. So . . . I . . . um . . . after a while, he wants more. Well, I didn't want to scare him off. I wanted him to be happy. I wanted him . . . to like me. Love me, maybe. I thought it would make me feel better when we . . . but I felt ashamed. I mean, I couldn't tell my mom. She . . . wouldn't understand how I could . . . well, I just didn't want her thinking bad about me. I was doing a good job'a that myself. And I didn't tell my friends—they expected we were doin' stuff anyways. I didn't have to say a thing. Well, somethin' I did must've spooked Teddy because he stopped calling. I scared 'im off. What an idiot! What was I supposed to say to him at school now? After what we did. Was I not good enough? Didn't I do things right? I should'a known what was coming, y'know! I COULD'A DONE SOMETHING ABOUT IT!

(She stops. She looks in a "mirror," touching her face. She gets furious.)

Great. Why didn't somebody tell me I had flour all over my face? I am a mess. I am such a mess. Look at me! *(Wipes her face)* I am such a geek! I showed him I cared for him, and he just walked out. I deserved it. I know I did. *(She stops. She turns off the radio. Pause.)* Then I started going out with Kevin. *(She starts eating another cookie.)* Kevin didn't have to tell me what to do. I was smart now. Y'know what I found out? You're gonna go at least as far with your new boyfriend as you did with your old one. And we did. Farther. I . . . just wanted him to . . . like me better than I liked me. Better than my mom liked me. Better than Teddy liked me. He kept talking like doin' it was no big deal. Casual. Natural. Unless I got squirrelly about it, then it was a very big deal. I just got tired of saying no all the time. I felt like

I was looking like a bigger jerk than I was. So we . . . it wasn't like a movie, I'll tell you that. Nothin' like it. Movies lie. They just lie, that's all. The media says, "Hey, it's exciting. It's going to make you feel great and loved and wanted." *(She picks up the last cookie.)* It's terrifying. It hurts. All the while, you wonder what he's thinkin' about you. Crazy stuff, like, do I look stupid right now? Is this the way I'm supposed to look? Is he gonna call me again if he doesn't like this? And, you get this little voice that says, does he even . . . appreciate this? Does this mean he loves me? Am I supposed to get, like . . . swept away in pleasure? What is this supposed to be all about? Kevin seemed to know. It's so strange, y'know. You think you're doin' right by saying no, then you find out that no is the wrong answer all of a sudden. *(Pause)* Everybody treats it like it's no big deal. But it is a big deal! *(Pause)* It was all mine, and I had the right to give it to whoever I wanted! Nobody had the right to just expect what's mine. Well, Kevin didn't think it was such a big deal, 'cuz—guess what—he broke up with me. It lasted a lot longer than Teddy. Oh, and he was way cool about it. He just graduated, going away to college, prob'ly, and didn't think a long-distance romance was gonna work. I saw him once more when he got back from some college prep summer school. He said he'd driven all day just to get back to see me 'cuz he missed me for some reason. I was . . . grateful. I was lonely. Someone missed me. I knew what I was supposed to do. And I did it.

(She notices the plate is empty. She picks it up and stares at it. She wipes the crumbs away.)

Who was I saving these for? I don't remember. Someone. *(She sighs.)* I feel sick. *(Pause for a moment, then the lights go to)*

(Blackout.)

Barre Exam

A Sketch for Three Girls on Self-esteem

Running Time

11 minutes

Scene

A dance studio. Day.

Cast

GIRL ONE: a high-school-age girl
GIRL TWO: a high-school-age girl
GIRL THREE: a high-school-age girl
ASSISTANT DIRECTOR: a young man or woman

Costume

Workout clothes (leotards, sweats, leg warmers, ballet shoes)
GIRL THREE wears very bright, funny-looking things.
ASSISTANT DIRECTOR wears nice slacks, shirt, and sweater.

Props

Bentwood chairs
Free-standing bulletin board covered with announcements
Ballet competition poster
Ballet exercise barre (large wooden dowel set up about waist high)
Rehearsal bags
Brightly colored, striped leg warmers
Glitter-ball antennae headband
Clipboard

Production Notes

Our idea for "Barre Exam" first came as a vision. We saw a young girl in workout clothes dancing around her father sitting in a chair. He did not or could not look at her. And she just kept moving around him, more and more desperate to get his attention.

And so the three young ballerinas in our sketch are performing, not for self-satisfaction or out of joy for a gift from God but to gain attention and acceptance from critical and emotionally distant parents. One girl actually believes her performance will make her feuding parents happy and so keep them together.

One of the important steps toward gaining self-esteem is learning you can't control what others feel or the decisions they make. Their approval and acceptance of you is not what life turns on.

The dialogue should flow seamlessly between the three main characters, since they are essentially telling the same tale. This is a very rhythmic sketch, in keeping with its metaphor. The ballet dancers need to make sure the space in front of them is understood to be a mirror, with small reactions to reflection to make that apparent. Nobody actually dances, but the warm-up exercises need to look real.

(A ballet studio. A few bentwood chairs scattered around. A small, free-standing bulletin board downstage. It is covered with torn odds and ends of announcements and news releases. A large readable poster says "BALLET COMPETITION AUDITIONS TODAY. OPEN TO THE PUBLIC." A ballet exercise barre is set up across the front of the stage. The audience is the "mirror" for the girls.

(The lights come up, as if turned on from the wall. Three GIRLS enter in workout clothes and carrying rehearsal bags. They smile tersely at one another, but there is no banter or overt friendliness between them.

(They start stretching and working out.)

GIRL ONE *(sitting on the ground and massaging her feet)*: Ohhh . . . my feet feel like I stood on razor blades all day. I'm telling you, they are just—

GIRL TWO *(stretching out on the floor)*: Killing me. My muscles are tighter than a drum. *(A litany as she twists her torso)* Sternocleidomastoid . . . deltoid . . . tricep . . . trapezius . . .

GIRL THREE: TA DA! *(Having already pulled on harlequin-striped leg warmers, a bright sweatshirt with a bizarre design, she has now dropped a pair of glitter-ball antennae on her head.)* Yes, yes, yes. *(Looks in the "mirror")* Works for me!

(ASSISTANT DIRECTOR walks in and hands everyone a typed sheet from a clipboard. He gives GIRL THREE a strange glance before he goes out.)

GIRLS: Just great. I'm in the first group up.

(They continue stretching.)

GIRL ONE: I'm going to have to be sharp. Come on, feet, don't fail me now. I've heard about middle-aged ballerinas, how their feet get all twisted and knotty from overwork. It doesn't matter, anyway. My pain doesn't matter. What's important is that they notice me. They have to notice me this time. I'll just die if they don't. I don't see how they can. They're always so distracted—writing, whispering, calling for more Perrier water. Looking at anything but me. *(She stands and begins to plié.)*

GIRL TWO *(bouncing on her outstretched legs)*: Sartorius . . . two, three, four . . . gracilis . . . two, three, four, five, six, seven, eight . . . Not one missed class . . . Two, three, four . . . adductor longus . . . five, six, seven, eight . . . gluteus medius . . . two, three, four . . . Not one missed workout . . . five, six, seven, eight . . . Not one mistake in an audition . . . *(slumps)* but it's never enough. It's never quite good enough for them. *(Shakes her shoulders back)* OK, OK, OK, OK. I'm OK. This'll be it. This'll be the one. This'll knock 'em to the floor. *(She stands and begins to plié.)*

GIRL THREE *(pulling off the antennae)*: Naaaah! I wish I had the guts to wear these. They'd fall out laughing. They'd get the biggest kick out of it, I know they would. *(Looks around)* Anybody'd laugh around here, their face would crack up. *(Laughs at her joke)* Maybe they need someone who could lighten things up around here. Take the falls and get the gags. I could do that. *(Starts to get up and does a big fall)* Nothin' hurts me. *(She stands and begins to move goofily.)*

(ASSISTANT DIRECTOR comes in.)

ASSISTANT DIRECTOR: Auditions start in five minutes. Have your résumés ready, please. *(He goes out.)*

(Small pause. All three GIRLS look into the "mirror" [toward audience].)

GIRL ONE: Wonder if he'll even remember to come and watch.

GIRL TWO: She'll be here. On the dot. Please like what you see this time.

GIRL THREE: They gotta show up. Last audition I made this bizarre face during the routine. They didn't fight for two days . . . just laughed about me.

(They work on basic exercise combinations.)

GIRL ONE: Last night I had this bad dream. I never sleep very well the night before an audition. I was standing next to my dad's chair. The one at the dinner table that he gives up only to my grandmother. Anyway, it was dinnertime. The table was set for everyone, but it was just me and him there. I was in my warm-up clothes, so I started doing combinations. He didn't notice me. Or wouldn't. I danced faster, what's the word? . . . exaggerated. But I could'a been doin' shadow puppets for Ray Charles. He didn't see me. He was watching TV. Some nature program. I fell to the ground. All of a sudden everyone was sitting around the table eating. I stayed on the floor.

GIRL TWO: This morning I woke up five minutes before my alarm. I was still caught in a dream, you know the kind you can't shake for about a minute. You think it really happened. Well, I walked into this theater. They were performing a musical, but I didn't recognize it. Suddenly somebody pushed me and said, "Your cue! You're late!" I was in my street clothes, but I jumped onto the stage. I panicked. I didn't know the choreography. I didn't know anything. I had to try and follow, but it was going too fast. Then I looked up. I saw my mother standing in the wings. She was horrified. Then I realized. It was her show. That's when the alarm went off.

GIRL THREE: This afternoon I fell asleep in American History class. I do it all the time. Postlunch Snicker's-bar crash. Anyway, the point is—and I don't want to sound all Shirley MacLaine or anything—but I had this sort-of vision. I was at a birthday party. I don't know whose. I was maybe six or seven. Everyone I knew was there, people I hadn't even met yet and ones I'd only seen in photos. Anyway, I was dressed in my mom's clothes. Lipstick, high heels, baggy nylons, the whole works. I was putting on a one-girl show, and everyone was laughing their heads off—except my mom and dad. They were crying. And the funnier I got, the more they cried. But I couldn't stop. And nothing, nothing I did could make them change.

(The music begins for the audition. The GIRLS look around, nervously.)

GIRL ONE: Where is . . . is that . . . ?

GIRL TWO: Maybe she . . . maybe . . .

GIRL THREE: Why don't they . . . are they . . . ?

GIRLS: THERE!

(GIRL ONE jumps up and waves wildly, like a kid in a Sunday School program. GIRL TWO draws up to full height and nods gracefully in greeting. GIRL THREE whistles with her fingers in her mouth and makes a funny face. Suddenly, they see each other. Intense embarrassment.)

GIRL ONE: My . . . ah, dad.

GIRL TWO: My mother.

GIRL THREE: Yeah . . . the parental units.

(They smile quickly, turning back to the "mirror." They stop. It's as if they see themselves for the first time. Things begin to click. After a moment, they look up.)

GIRL ONE: Father, they're all performing for someone else too.

GIRL TWO: Unbelievable. God, why do we spend so much time dancing for other people?

GIRL THREE: Lord, am I really responsible to make them have a good time?

GIRL ONE: Do I have to work so hard to interest them?

GIRL TWO: Please them?

GIRL THREE: Entertain them?

GIRL ONE: For once, I'd just like to . . . dance for myself.

GIRL TWO: Succeed for myself.

GIRL THREE: Please myself.

(ASSISTANT DIRECTOR *comes in.*)

ASSISTANT DIRECTOR: You three are on. *(He goes out.)*

(They watch him go out, then turn back to the "mirror" and continue their prayer.)

GIRL ONE: Lord, I know You're interested in me.

GIRL TWO: You approve of me.

GIRL THREE: You enjoy me.

GIRLS: And I don't even have to perform. *(They look out to the audience.)* Here I go. *(They turn to one another.)* Good luck.

(Blackout.)

Scars

A Monologue Series on the Pain That Binds Us

Running Time

18 minutes

Scene

A stage. Any time.

Cast

CHEERLEADER: a high-school-age girl
ARTIST: a high-school-age guy or girl
PLAYBOY: a high-school-age guy
JOCK: a high-school-age guy
LONER: a high-school-age guy or girl
HOMECOMING QUEEN: a high-school-age girl
REBEL: a high-school-age girl
DRUM MAJOR: a high-school-age guy or girl
CLASS CLOWN: a high-school-age guy
VALEDICTORIAN: a high-school-age guy or girl
SCIENCE CLUB PRESIDENT: a high-school-age guy
PARTY ANIMAL: a high-school-age guy

Costume

Modern. Costumes can reflect and illustrate each character stereotype, or you can use casual dress that allows the signs around the necks only to identify the stereotypes.

Props

12 folding chairs
Around-the-neck signs that say CHEERLEADER, JOCK, etc.

Production Notes

There is a party game you might have played. One person begins a story and the next takes it up until it winds its often outrageous way around the room.

That's the idea behind "Scars." A group of high school types—cheerleader, class clown, science club president, etc.—tell the story of their pain. One begins and each adds his portion, which is made more and more remarkable, not by how strange and wild the story gets but by the fact that they share so much in common, despite their status and role in high school society.

In the end, we discover these teens are who they are in part because of their scars—their pain. But they are becoming who they are in Christ because of the healing of Jesus of Nazareth.

We thought of "Scars" as being useful in several ways. If you want a complete spectrum of issues, then the entire play would offer just that. Each monologue, in effect, can stand alone, as well. You could use them separately to deal with a specific topic, or hitch a few together for a smaller scale production. The monologues aren't really designed to provide answers but are portraits of reality meant to open up discussion.

In addition, if you don't want to perform "Scars," you can break it up as reading material in a youth group meeting, inviting comments afterward. Different people could be chosen to read each character.

If you decide to do the entire play, remember that the segues from one character to the next have to have the precision of a finely tuned relay race. One character takes the story baton from the next. Be careful not to have the characters know another is standing next to them until the final moment.

(12 teenagers sit on folding chairs or on the floor all around the playing area. Around each neck is hung a sign: CHEERLEADER, ARTIST, PLAYBOY, JOCK, LONER, HOMECOMING QUEEN, REBEL, DRUM MAJOR, CLASS CLOWN, VALEDICTORIAN, SCIENCE CLUB PRESIDENT, *and* PARTY ANIMAL.

(Each one comes forward, carrying on the story the one before has begun. Once their story is told, they remain standing, creating a tableaux by the scene's end.

("CHEERLEADER" *starts off. She stands and moves to the downstage right front of the stage. She shields her eyes, looking out into the audience, straining to see.)*

CHEERLEADER: Did you ask me if I liked myself? *(Listens)* Oh. Well . . . yeah. Yeah, I do. Being a senior has been the best. I'm sure the team is going to go downstate this year. We'll get to do our stuff in front of, like, thousands of people, plus television cameras and everything. Huh? Yeah, I guess I'm a little nervous about it. I never used to get nervous. You know, I started cheering when I was a sophomore, ah, but before that I wanted to be a gymnast. Yeah, lessons at the Y and private lessons and stuff. I had real Nadia fantasies, y'know. Maybe because my first coach was this gigantic Russian who would call us his babushkas when we hit our marks but went off on us if we made a mistake. Any mistake. Like a maniac in this foreign language for anything. And I sure made my share of mistakes . . . *(Lost in thought a moment)* Yeah, I'm really nervous I'm going to blow it on national TV. My mom, of course, will be so kind as to point it out the second I get home. "Hi, honey, why are you such a geek?" I guess I was born such a major klutz. I could just die—

("ARTIST" *stands on his first word, seamlessly finishing* "CHEERLEADER's" *last sentence. He joins her at the front of the stage. As he speaks,* "CHEERLEADER" *turns her head to listen to* "ARTIST" *and silently holds her left hand out to him. He doesn't notice her.)*

ARTIST *(standing):* In advance. I mean the whole project. I had it done two weeks early so I could get some feedback and change something before it was too late. I mean, this wasn't a citywide competition like I'd been in before. We're talking Washington, D.C. Smithsonian. College bucks. It was all I did all semester. Algebra, Spanish, American lit., all of it down the tubes for this baby. So, one day during study hall I finally get up enough courage to go down to 101 to see what my art teacher thinks about it, and way before I get there I hear this whole class laughing their guts out. The door's open and I see this . . . crummy teacher showing my piece to the class as an example of what *not* to enter. Oh, it was all a big hoot. He never said a word to me. Never even gave me a chance. And you know the saddest part? I thought he liked me. Man, I have never felt so . . . alone—

("PLAYBOY" *stands on his first word, finishing* "ARTIST's" *last sentence and joins the others at the front of the stage.* "ARTIST" *holds out his hand to* "PLAYBOY" *as* "CHEERLEADER" *did.* "PLAYBOY" *doesn't notice him. This pattern gets repeated down the line as each new speaker comes forward.)*

PLAYBOY *(standing):* In all my life. I mean, I really liked this girl. Big time. I have this . . . reputation around school, and not without some reasons, y'know. But I thought I would clean up the act. I started comin' down on people getting all squirrelly and talkin' gross around her. I really tried to treat her nice, and I didn't push her or anything. So, at this party, she gets all wired and tells me I'm not the major hunk she thought I was. Where's Mr. Macho? I mean, what a bim! She liked what she thought I was. I never had a chance. So I blitz out of this party and take a walk to figure this out, and to keep from getting really mad and doin' something I'd regret. I come home, and my dad's waiting up for me, already with a buzz on, like usual. He's hacked because I did something stupid—oh, I left the milk out and it went bad or something lame like that. He busts me one. Bam! Before I have the chance to say a thing, it's over, y'know? That's the way my dad ends all his sentences. Knuckle punctuation. I went into the bathroom to see if my—

(Same business as above)

JOCK *(standing):* Nose was broken. We were just wrestling around in the front room. I don't know how it happened, but all'a sudden we're both goin' for it. I was already ticked about missing a pass at Tuesday's game. My little brother's small, but the dude's wiry. He's all over ya. I couldn't pin 'em for the life'a me, and I'm gettin' more and more bent and finally I just popped him. I bit down hard and threw one. Broke his nose. I could've killed myself. The whole thing looked too familiar. My big brother—he's married now— he use'ta come home after he lost a little league game and wait for me to say something to him, and he'd come at me, fists flyin'. Black-eye city every couple'a weeks. Told my parents it was this guy at school that was doin' it. My dad must've dropped a couple'a thousand dollars on boxing and karate lessons for me. Paid off, I guess. I can break my little brother's nose. I've also got my share of block letters. I'm a natural, that's all. But that isn't enough sometimes. Last week, my running partner tells me he's been doin' steroids all year. He's pumped, that's for sure. And the dude is way fast. And . . . I'm thinkin' maybe I could use the help. You can't be just good to get anywhere anymore. You have to be the best. And I was thinkin', maybe I need to be—

(Same business as above)

LONER *(standing):* Better than I am. More . . . interesting. Not so terrified of what people think. What I think of myself, I guess. Anyway, that's why I started smoking dope with 'em all. And drinking. You couldn't be part of 'em unless you did, and they looked like the only people who even wanted me around. There wasn't a question of just saying no. The correct answer was "sure." And when I was toasted, I liked me better. I didn't act like me. I wasn't afraid. After I started partying, I became, like, someone else. And I'd wonder, is this bold, likable person really me, or am I just "Jack Daniels"? But then it'd wear off, or I'd wake up in the hallway or something, and I'd start hugging the walls again. Doin' what they do is not what I want out of life. *(Stops)* I'm not sure. What do I want out of life? You can believe nobody'd understand what I wanted even if I had someone to tell. Maybe keeping it to yourself is way better than the blank stares you get when you try to explain anything. Man, the way my parents stare at me is the worst. Sometimes when I try to explain who I am my mom's mouth drops so far open—

(Same business as above)

HOMECOMING QUEEN *(standing):* This hugeoid glob of fiber-bran tofu oatmeal cake falls in her lap. I had to repeat myself about nine times. "Homecoming Queen, Mom. I JUST GOT VOTED IN AS HOMECOMING QUEEN!" Well, you'd think I'd just told her I personally signed up to slaughter the last, living endangered humpback whale. Her mouth hung open. How could something so exciting to me be so shameful to her? Shameful, that's exactly the word she used. "You should be ashamed of yourself for wanting to be a part of something so degrading to women." Then she just went right on talking to my dad about some Amnesty International protest she was going to. What does she know about what's shameful and what's the most exciting thing that has ever happened in my life? Degrading. I'll tell . . . you want to know what I think is degrading? The way my friends adjust their morals for every new boyfriend they get. And I get degraded because I'm not going to sleep with anyone but my husband. "You're missing out on what it means to be a woman," they're all telling me. They're as bad as my mom. Everybody's got her own ideas about how to be a woman. Well, I am definitely a woman. But I want to do it—

(Same business as above)

REBEL *(standing):* My own way. OK, so maybe I do have my own way of doing things. I feel like barfing anytime I do anything close to the way other people do things. So does that make me a candidate for continuation school or something? So, I don't like to follow the crowd, and, man, do the stories fly about me. They get all twisted around until I've got this reputation'a doin' things I never even thought of. I mean, last week I walked up behind these "ladies" in the bathroom fixing their . . . I don't know, lipgloss or somethin' and they're gabbin' about some airhead with no morals partying with every guy around. Well, it finally dawns on me that it's *me* they're talkin' about. I straightened them out big time. Good thing I do things the way I want to. I never want to be what people expect me to be, because nobody else ever seems to turn out to be what I expected them to be. Like my parents, for example. I expected them to be husband and wife. Well, they're doing things their own way. Last week I hear the news. They're splitting up—

(Same business as above)

DRUM MAJOR *(standing):* And they sure have been quiet about it. I'm exhausted anyway. I felt so . . . responsible for their happiness and their relationship for so long. I've been talking to this counselor on Fridays during my study hall who's helped me see I've been doing things all my life to keep them together. Even the band. The State Competition. They both flew down after work to see us gig. I looked up into the stands afterward and I was feeling hot! We totally capped on every other school. My folks were really easy to spot. They had on these matching sweatshirts with "Gig It!" written on 'em and made in our school colors. My friends think they are the perfect parents of all time. And even I thought everything'd be OK after that for some strange reason. I didn't even know they'd already filed for divorce. I don't know what I'm doing anymore. I don't know who I want to live with. I wanna live with both of 'em! Together in the same house. I don't want things the way they are. At all. They probably never even considered me when they signed those stupid papers. Who really cares anyway? Maybe they think I'll fade away. They obviously don't need me. What's the point now—

(Same business as above)

CLASS CLOWN *(standing)*: Of living. I've thought about that a lot lately. I mean, high school's supposed to be the easy part of life. *(With Australian accent)* "No worries, mate." Worries start up when you leave school and go out into the big, scary world, right? Well, if this isn't scary, I'd hate to see what things're like when I hit the pavement. What could be worse than having to get up before noon to watch Mr. Fenswick's lecture with that white stuff in the corner of his mouth. That's scary. Hey, whadd'ya call 10 vice principals at the bottom of the Pacific Ocean? A start. *(Makes a drum rimshot)* They get better after I've had lunch. A school lunch. Y'know, "I'll have some yellow stuff, some brown stuff, and some of that . . . that . . . what *is* that stuff, anyway? Gimme two helpings. Oh, and after the mystery meat there's always driver's ed with those thumbs-up movies. *(Raises hand)* "Oh, please, can we see 'Blood Highway' again? No, no, I *want* to lose my lunch." *(Pause)* I like it when people laugh. For a split second, I don't feel afraid. Then when it's over, I feel panic set in. I'm afraid of how afraid I feel. You're not supposed to feel afraid in high school, are you? Hey, did you hear about the atheist lying in his coffin? Yeah, all dressed up and—

(Same business as above)

VALEDICTORIAN *(standing)*: Nowhere to go. I mean, nowhere. Finals and SATs just around the corner, and the colleges I applied to are doing these major entrance exams. I feel like I'm trapped, like I can't breathe. Like I'm crawling out of my skin. I know the official name for it. I went to the library last Saturday and looked up some articles on it in *Psychology Today*. Performance anxiety. Panic attack syndrome. Anxiety disorders. It feels massively creepy to read about yourself in articles by Ph.D.s and directors of psychiatry hospitals. But it happens to me everywhere. World history presentation, vocabulary tests, answering a basic trig equation. My heart races, my stomach closes up, the sweat pours, and I feel like bolting for the door. And everybody thinks it's so easy for me—a shoo-in for valedictorian. I should be calm and collected. But I'm not going to make it through grad school without a triple bypass at this rate. I'm so terrified of failing. Last week we had a quiz in biology. A stupid little quiz, but I couldn't bring myself to study for it. I got an "F," of course. My one and only of all time. But there's no way I can tell anyone about this failure thing—

(Same business as above)

SCIENCE CLUB PRESIDENT *(standing)*: At least no one in this new school will ever know about it. I've completely changed my life. I'm just a lot more careful now, you see? I don't *even* attempt things I'm not absolutely positive I'm going to ace. But that makes anything close to scientific research and study a big-time joke. I don't care. I'm just glad to be out of that other school and town. For some people, blowing up an entire section of their school might be a reason to party, but for me it was total humiliation. The whole science fair had to be relocated to the elementary school gymnasium. Several entries, including mine as you probably figured out, were completely wasted. I was hated more than Bulbhead Bowman, the vice principal. It was like a pardon when my dad got a promotion and had to transfer. My mom thought I was such a good-natured kid for having the courage to leave my friends so close to graduation. Get out. What friends? I blew them all off. Well my project did, anyway. Nobody in the science club even talked to me anymore. So, I've decided not to make any friends here either. That way, there's less people to disappoint, and who'll turn on you. I'm not saying it isn't lonely and that I don't miss people, all I'm saying is it's just not—

(Same business as above)

PARTY ANIMAL *(standing):* Worth the risk, y'know? You get close to people, then you have to tell 'em stuff about yourself. Well, they expect it. It's part'a the deal of friendship. Well, once they know about you, they can use it against ya. So I'll party with 'em. That doesn't mean a thing. Everyone's your best friend when you're wasted, right? And I don't mean to say I'm alone. Dude, I got people around me night and day. I'm just not going to let any of 'em get to know me. People are way dorked, anyways. I mean, they really believe that this emptiness inside, they really think other people can fill that spot. What a joke, right? A girlfriend? Get out. A best bud? Not even close. Right now, Olde English 800 and Henry the Bong are hitting the spot. Or maybe I'm just forgetting the spot is there. That's prob'ly more like it. I guess I can't speak for anyone but me, but does everyone have such a hole inside his skin? Is it like . . . a deformity or what? Something that didn't develop right inside'a Mommie Dearest? Why do I feel it? Is there anyone who can fix it? *(Small pause)* What? Yeah, sure . . . *(Digs in his pocket)* . . . Mr. Joint coming right up.

(They freeze. Then they all look up at the audience in unison. "PARTY ANIMAL" looks to his right and sees the "SCIENCE CLUB PRESIDENT," who is holding out his left hand to him. "PARTY" gives him a look like, "You've got to be kidding?" Then he looks down the line of people, looking at him. Something clicks. He takes the hand of "PRESIDENT." The same thing happens between "PRESIDENT" and "VALEDICTORIAN," and so on down the line, one at a time, each reacting to the next person in disbelief, initial disgust, uncertainty, etc., according to their character. Finally, they are all holding hands. They look up at the audience.)

UNISON: Our scars. Sometimes they match up. Sometimes they help us recognize each other. Sometimes we find out they're still open wounds. But any way you look at it, we all need to be healed.

("PARTY ANIMAL" steps forward. He removes his sign.)

PARTY ANIMAL: When Thomas first heard that Jesus had risen from the dead, he wanted to touch His scars. They were the proof that He had suffered. They were the proof Jesus was who He said He was.

("CHEERLEADER" *steps forward. She removes her sign.*)

CHEERLEADER: Even Jesus had scars. He doesn't promise we won't get a few. He just promises that we don't have to wear them all by ourselves. We have someone who knows about them . . . firsthand . . . on our side.

("LONER" *steps forward. She removes her sign.*)

LONER: And we have each other. Our scars don't match up for nothing. It is His promise of understanding and a visible sign that we are not alone.

(*The lights fade to*)

(*Blackout.*)